LAYS IN SUMMER LANDS

J. Willis Menard

JOHN WILLIS MENARD

LAYS IN SUMMER LANDS

Edited by

Larry Eugene Rivers
Richard Mathews
Canter Brown Jr.

UNIVERSITY OF TAMPA PRESS
TAMPA, FLORIDA
2002

The original text first entered according to Act of Congress in the year 1879
by J. Willis Menard
in the Office of the Librarian of Congress, at Washington, D.C.

New preface, essays, notes, and accompanying materials
Copyright © 2002 by Larry E. Rivers, Richard Mathews, and Canter Brown Jr.
Cover design by Ana Montalvo from an 1871 engraving

Manufactured in the United States of America
Printed on acid free paper ∞
First Edition

The University of Tampa Press
401 West Kennedy Boulevard
Tampa, Florida 33606

ISBN 1-879852-74-8

Library of Congress Cataloging-in-Publication Data

Menard, John Willis, 1838-1893.
    Lays in summer lands / John Willis Menard ; edited by Larry Eugene
Rivers, Richard Mathews, Canter Brown, Jr.
        p. cm.
    ISBN 1-879852-74-8 (hardcover : alk. paper)
    1. African Americans—Poetry.   I. Rivers, Larry E., 1950-   .
II. Mathews, Richard, 1944-   . III. Brown, Canter. IV. Title.
PS2389.M2L39 2002
811'.4—dc21   2001007367

⁘ Contents ⁘

John Willis Menard receives congratulations from his friends on the floor of the U.S. House of Representatives on December 7, 1868, following his election as the nation's first black congressman.

Preface

John Willis Menard ranks among the most important and yet little-known black leaders and intellectuals of his era. He could claim credit, after all, as the first man of his race ever elected to the United States Congress. Yet, even though the names of many African Americans and the substance of their accomplishments easily come to mind, few people know of or have found cause to reflect upon Menard's political career during this period. Fewer still know of his contributions to literature–particularly his poetry. Scholars have focused on the writings of such famous individuals as Frederick Douglass, Henry McNeal Turner, William Wells Brown, Frances Ellen Watkins Harper, Booker T. Washington, and Harriet E. Wilson, just to mention a few. Menard's legacy, though, essentially has been forgotten.

The rare mentions of Menard's name have come over the years within narrow points of focus. When people have considered him, they usually have thought within the context of black state legislators during Reconstruction. Black politicians of that time usually proved capable, helping to do what they could to uplift poor whites and former slaves. After Reconstruction's end, however, political options grew fewer, increasingly circumscribed by local power brokers and the stark realities of racial discrimination. By the early twentieth century, Menard, like many other black politicians of his time, represented an era that many whites preferred to forget.

Menard died in 1893, and after so many years, no comprehensive biography of him yet has been written. A few articles mention his political career, but no study focuses on his writings. His one book, *Lays in Summer Lands*, published in 1879, failed to establish him as a leading poet of his generation. Today he remains all but unknown within the very region where he lived and wrote. On the other hand, his poems reflect his brilliance, insights, life experiences, and society in complex and artful ways. He gives poetic voice to a geographic and cultural terrain of great importance, one under-represented by an early Southern literary canon now restricted primarily to George Washington Cable and Kate Chopin (New Orleans), Joel Chandler Harris (Eatonton and Atlanta, Georgia), and Sidney Lanier (Macon, Georgia). Not only does Menard's writing encompass a unique grouping of regions (a broad rectangle from Illinois to New Orleans, the Caribbean, Florida, and Washington, D.C.), but he writes of minority experience with eloquence, passion, humor, sensitivity, and grace.

Convinced that Menard's poems offer a window to view his time's history, culture, and geography—as well as a remarkable human being—the editors present *Lays in Summer Lands* for others to read and enjoy. We have appended essays to help place the work within historical and literary contexts and to offer critical perspectives that we hope will begin to convey the value and merit we have found in this book. Explanatory notes, located as specified in the table of contents, will clarify historical references and unfamiliar usage of words in some of the poems. Finally, indexes to titles, first lines, and names and subjects provide access to the poems and commentary. Readers should note that certain material regarding Menard's political career that appeared in the original edition has been omitted here.

John Willis Menard speaks for himself, but the first edition of his book featured a preface by the prominent black leader Frederick G. Barbadoes, who associated in anti-slavery and civil rights work with Frederick Douglass, Robert Purvis, George T. Downing, Alexander Crummell, and other influential figures of the day. His father James G. Barbadoes had been a signer of the declaration of principles of the Anti-Slavery Society in Philadelphia during 1833, and Frederick, after striking out for California during the Gold Rush and earning financial independence, spent his money freely to support Abolitionist and other worthy causes. Barbadoes knew Menard well, and his preface articulates the importance this exemplary man held for those who came to know him and his work. We trust you, too, will be rewarded by making his acquaintance.

–*Larry Eugene Rivers, Richard Mathews, and Canter Brown Jr.*
Tallahassee and Tampa, 2002

Preface to the 1879 Edition

The millions of Negroes in this country, and their right of suffrage, will count but little in their history without proportionate and conspicuous brain power; for it is cultivated intellect that commands respect, disarms prejudice, and forces itself to the front rank of majestic manhood. Our race can only succeed in winning a place in history by cultivating a pride of race through a high order of character and education, and by commemorating such notable events and deeds during their existence as are calculated to claim the attention of future historians and the reverence of their posterity; for a race will be remembered only by its *deeds*, and not by its condition and numbers.

The grand results of the war are: Freedom to the slave, the right of suffrage, and the privilege to hold office. To justify these results, and the hopes of the friends of freedom, the Negro had a grave responsibility on his shoulders. If he began with credit to his race, (his opportunities considered), well and good; but if he fell short of what was reasonably expected of him, his friends in the North might have felt disgusted and probably forsaken him. Congress, the great arena of the nation, was the only place where the American people and the world could see him and test his abilities and manhood.

Mr. Menard, being the first of his race elected to Congress, represented not only his race, but the immediate results of the war. His position was a trying one; and that he acquitted himself with credit and marked ability, the [complimentary] notices of the press of the country fully attest.

Mr. Menard was born in Kaskaskia, Illinois, and his parents were descendants of colored Creole French of New Orleans. During the war he came to Washington, and entered the emigration field, was appointed as a clerk in the Bureau of Emigration, Interior Department. This was the first time a Negro held a clerkship in the Government service. He went to British Honduras in 1863, with a view of founding a colony of colored emigrants from this country. On his return, he made a report to President Lincoln, which was published. In 1865 he went to New Orleans and was soon after appointed Inspector of Customs. He was subsequently appointed one of the Street Commissioners of that city. He published two papers there—first the *Free South*, and afterwards the *Radical Standard*. He was nominated for Congress in 1868, receiving twenty-two votes out of a convention of thirty delegates, and declared elected by the proper authorities of the State. Mr. Menard ran for an unexpired term of the Fortieth Congress, and General [Lionel Allen] Sheldon ran on the same ticket for the Forty-first Congress. Both received the same vote, and both were elected by the same State authority.

The fact that General Sheldon was seated and Menard not, proves very fully that his color kept him out. However, he received the same pay ($2,500) as he would have been given had he been seated. He broke the ice, however, for others of his race to follow.

Mr. Menard removed to Florida in 1871, and published a paper there called *The Sun*. He was appointed a clerk in the Postoffice at Jacksonville; and while in that position was elected to the Legislature. After serving out his term, he was appointed a Collector of Internal Revenue, and also, afterwards, was twice appointed Justice of the Peace. In 1876 he was elected a delegate to the National Republic Convention at Cincinnati.

In all of these public trusts—many of them of great importance—he proved himself capable and faithful, and retired from them without a stain on his official integrity.

For these brave and determined efforts to prove the ability of his race, he deserves their approval, and that of every true lover of justice and equality; and I am sure that none will hesitate to award him the merit he deserves, or deny him the place in history to which he is justly entitled.

—F.G. Barbadoes
Washington, D.C.
October 5, 1879.

POEMS.

To President Lincoln

On issuing the Emancipation Proclamation

THOU hast spoken! —Let the earth resound
    With hallelujahs to our gracious God!—
The gladsome news—four million men will soon
    No longer groan beneath the tyrant's rod!

Thy words are echoed by ten million hearts
    From hill to dale—to the islands of the sea:
They are Redemption's chartered harbingers,
    When men—no longer slaves, but free shall be!

Thou hast spoken! and a million arms
    Are gleaming brightly from the battle van;
And banners proudly waving on the breeze—
    Presaging victory to thy ripening plan!

Thou hast spoken! and thy name shall glow
    Forever on Columbia's altar bright;
For thou hast stayed a vile, despotic tide,
    And bravely battled for the trampled right!

May thy footsteps ever lead thee upward—
    Upward to that bright, celestial land:
Where safely sheltered from the storms of life,
    Thou'lt join the heroes of the Patriots' band.

Grant's First Election

ONCE more, O harp! let me gentle touch
 Thy thrilling numbers soft and sweet—
Once more with new-born energies
 The King of Liberty to greet!
   With joy complete,
   And hope replete,
  Thy notes of triumph now repeat!

All hail the Chief! the good, the great—
 The new-made King of Liberty!
Let cannon, bell, and trumpet sound,
 From mountain, valley, plain, and sea!
   And Dark and Light
   No longer fight,
  For Wrong has yielded unto Right!

From icy North to sunny South,
 Let the proud flag of Freedom wave!
Let its broad, starry folds, unfurled,
 The storms of dark Oppression brave!
   For Heaven gave
   No man a slave
  The sweets of Liberty to crave!

This land is Freedom's heritage—
 The home of Liberty and Peace;
And Treason, with its fiendish deeds,
 In the fair, sunny South, shall cease;
   And God to Thee,
   We bend our knee,
  And thank Thee for our victory!

The Wife's Invocation

"LOVE me, leave me not" —no never,
    Life is dark and full of woe;
We are one and cannot sever,
    Though the winds of sorrow blow!
True, I often sigh in sorrow—
    Sigh because your words are cold;
But the sunshine of the morrow,
    Fills my heart with joy untold.

"Love me, leave me not," for dreary
    Are the days when you're away;
And my heart grows sick and weary,
    As I vainly sigh and pray.
Once a warm love cheer'd my bosom,
    When our years were young and gay;
Now 'tis faded—but 'twill blossom,
    When this long night turns to day!

"Love me, leave me not," in anguish,
    Press your warm lips into mine;
Then this heart no more will languish,
    If again you call me thine.
We have kiss'd and truly given
    Vows before the sacred shrine;
And we're one on earth—in Heaven—
    You are mine and I am thine!

Love me—claim this aching bosom,
    Press it once more to thine own!
And the flow'rs of Hope will blossom
    Where the pangs of sorrow burn!

Take me, I am thine forever—
  Soon from earth we'll pass away;
But we'll meet, when here we sever,
  In a brighter land of day.

To E.M.T., of Jamaica

AWAY from thy green island home,
   From beneath thy blue tropic skies;
Thou sendest me missives to come,
   Where the hue of the rose never dies.

If thy soft, gentle spirit now pines,
   For a form that is now far away;
I will send you these few simple lines,
   To beguile the long weary day.

Thy friendship, though young, I will keep,
   And its ties I will try to improve,
Till like wand'ring vines they will creep,
   Upon the famed bower of love!

Thy mem'ry like a bright sunny beam,
   Lingers near me by day and by night,
Like the swift fairy pinion and gleam,
   Of a heavenly vision of light!

Fare thee well in thy sweet island home,
   Till the one who is far from thee now,
Again to thy bosom shall come,
   With kisses so sweet for thy brow!

First Sabbath of the Year

ALMIGHTY God of love divine,
    Fill us anew with love and fear,
While we now worship at Thy shrine,
    This first sweet Sabbath of the year!

We've wander'd from Thy paths of Right,
    And tread the thorny walks of Sin,
Which lead us from thy heavenly light
    That gives such endless joy within!

Oh, Father, pity and forgive
    Such erring children as we are!
Thy love, oh give us—lest we live
    Forevermore in black despair!

A *New Year* now, with radiant light,
    Bids us be loving and sincere,
While we now pledge the paths of Right
    To humbly walk throughout the year.

Then fill us with Thy love divine,
    Great Ruler of the starry sphere!
And softly whisper "We are thine,"
    This first bright Sabbath of the year!

Stanzas on Cuba

UNFURL once more the banner of the free,
   And on to Cuba with songs of liberty!
Four hundred thousand men are still in chain
   Beneath the galling yoke of cruel Spain.

Reach out, Columbia! thy powerful hand,
   And aid the struggling Patriots' band,
Who for long, gloomy years of fire and blood,
   Against the savage hordes of Spain have stood.

Reach out, and teach the buccaneers of Spain
   That slaves no more can breathe near thy domain;
And that henceforth the Western Hemisphere,
   No more the clanking chains of slaves shall hear.

Poor, bleeding isle! take hope: despotic Spain
   Must soon release thee from her galling chain;
Her madness and the murders of her bands,
   Are the last links that bind thy suppliant hands.

Unfurl the dear old flag, with joyful songs,
   And on to Cuba to right the Patriots' wrongs;
Come war or peace, that island must be free,
   The jig is up, all hail the jubalee!

Just over the Sea

Just over the sea,
   In a green sunny isle,
Lives a maiden whose smile
   Is sunlight to me.

She's a sweet, fairy one,
   Whose soft, mellow voice,
Has made me rejoice
   In hours that are gone.

Her footsteps, so light—
   With tresses that curl,
And fine teeth of pearl,
   With eyes quite as bright.

My heart to her flows
   With pure, simple love,
Like rain from above,
   Wherever she goes.

Just over the sea
   Is the girl of my choice,
Whose angel-like voice
   Is music to me!

Though cares may betide,
   I'll soon call her *my wife*,
Through all coming life,
   And stay by her side!

Estella

In Honduras, 1863

THE sun was high in the torrid skies, his westward
    course pursuing,
While fell in profusion his golden rays on the vernal
    fields of Honduras.
The crystal dew of the rosy morn, in the cups of the
    flowers still linger'd,
While their odor sweet, that freighted the air, perfumed
    the murmering zephyrs.
The sportive birds, with their plummage rare, in the air,
    their course were winging,
While fell on the ear, their merry songs, like the notes
    of the flute on the waters!
'TWAS on a morning like this that I were to set out,
    with a skillful band of explorers,
For the far-off western hills and dales in the vernal wilds
    of Honduras.
After freighting our proud and restless boat, with luggage,
    provisions, utensils,
We spread her snowy wings to the wind, and sailed
    up the coast of Honduras!
Bright was the scene on the coast when we saw, as we
    wung o'er the heads of the surges,
While the hue of the sylvan isles that we pass'd, seemed to
    rival the blue in the waters.
Calmly, silently, the day wore on—like the monotonous
    voice of the breakers,
Till twilight came with a noiseless step and threw her pall
    o'er the waters.
The stars bowed low when their mother moon rose up
    in the glittering heavens.

THEN followed her westward on her silver tract, like
children following their mother.
Noiselessly, lonely, the night wore on, till the rays of the
morning descended,
On the far-off drifting eastern clouds, like the smiles of a
bride on her husband!
At anchor, we leisurely, merrily rode, right in front of an
ancient village,
While our cook, in rudely, hunter style, our morning
refreshments was serving.
The rays of the tropic sun dispersed the clouds on the
eastern horizon,
Then fell on the shrubbery, the houses and water, like the
drops of the dew on the flowers.
Then my guide and myself started off, in a red canoe
for the landing,
And like lost sheep we strolled along through the grassy
streets of the village.
Sweet and bright were the scenes that we saw, as we
walked up the streets of the village,
But sweeter by far, were the starry eyes and angel-forms
of the maidens!
Especially one—Estella—the queen, and belle of that
tropical village;
The ray of whose humid eyes, I ween, could have wooed
an angel from heaven!
Her bosom heaved, her eyes spoke love, and her hair, like
the wing of a raven,
And happy was he, who could touch her hand or *even* the
hem of her garment!
My eyes were filled with unshed tears, when I heard on
the eave of the morrow,
Estella, the queen, was to be *a bride*, and would sail on
the sea with her *husband!*

Florida

SWEET ocean goddess, divinely fair and free,
Outstretching far into the summer sea,

As if to catch the constant ocean breeze
That swiftly speeds over the gulf and seas!

Thou art a fairy land—a "Land of Flowers,"
With towering pines and vine-clad bowers—

With boundless lakes and broad, majestic streams,
That bask forever in bright, sunny gleams.

Dear sunny land of orange and balmy sky,
Where summer reigns and flowers never die!

Thrice bless'd art thou, with trees forever green,
And varied fruit, with air and clime serene.

Long hast thou groaned 'neath burdens of the Past,—
Ravaged by wars and by oppression blast:

But now take hope—thy future shall be bright,
Thy chains have fallen, and ended is thy night.

Thy wasted fields and trees will yield again:
Redoubled harvests shall thy sons regain.

Thy hidden wealth, and healing balmy clime,
And charming scenery, varied and sublime,

Must lure from every clime, from every land,
Uncounted thousands to thy shores of sand.

And these will summon forth, with skilful toil,
The hidden treasures of thy wasted soil.

Take hope and rise, land of the fig and pine!
Thy woes are ended and new life is thine.

Labor and Liberty, and wealth and power,
Henceforth will be thy allotted dower!

Waiting at Live Oak

Live Oak, Fla., a junction

Of all the minor woes,
A mortal undergoes,
'Tis waiting in shawl or cloak
Seven hours at Live Oak!

Waiting from nine to four,
Seven hours, sometimes more,
Amid box-cars and logs,
And the music of the frogs.

Musquitos, bugs and fleas,
Vile dust or raging seas,
Inflict, by far, less pain,
Than waiting for a train.

Ye gods of Rome and Greece,
When shall this waiting cease—
This waiting in the cold and rain
For the Savannah train!

I'd much prefer to take
A ride o'er Great Salt Lake—
The mountains of the moon,
Or to the grand Ty-coon,

Than wait in rain or cold,
With minor woes untold,
Wrapp'd up in shawl or cloak,
Seven hours at Live Oak!

Sabbath Eve Musings

THE Sabbath bells—how sweet their chime!
  Now floating on the air,
Calling, with solemn tones sublime,
  Souls to the house of prayer.

Sweet heavenly music, float along,
  Upon the air of even;
Thy notes invite the careless throng
  From sinful paths to heaven!

I'm all alone this Sabbath eve,
  Pondering o'er the past—
The faded past that makes me grieve
  For joys that could not last.

Come back to me, ye faded forms,
  This sad, sweet Sabbath night;
Though faded, yet your memory charms
  Like rays of heavenly light!

O, floating memories ever dear,
  Why do ye make me sad?
Why do ye woo the silent tear
  From eyes that would be glad?

Ye dragging hours of woe and gloom,
  Freighted with toil and care:
Driving the light from out my room,
  And leaving dark despair!

The West wind groans against the door,
   The fire has lost its glow;
My faithful lamp, with green shade o'er,
   Burns silently and low.

And so with me, I'm waning too—
   I'm feeling tired of life;
Sweet sleep and rest my eyelids woo—
   Farewell to daily strife!

A Glance

Is THY name Mary, maiden fair?
    Such should, I think, its music be;
The sweetest name that women bear
    Were best befitting thee;
And she, to whom it once was given,
    Was half of earth and half of heaven.

I hear thy voice, I see thy smile,
    I look upon thy folded hair;
Ah! while I dream not they beguile,
    My heart is in the snare;
And she, who chains a wild bird's wing,
    Must start not if her captive sing!

Musings

THE gentle moon now silvers
    The bosom of the sea,
While zephyrs make the forest
    Resound with melody!

I set me down to ponder
    Beside this moonlit stream;
And while I muse, sweet Luna
    Will cheer me with her beam.

My brow is dimmed with memories
    Of faded joys of yore—
Of one who now is winging
    Upon the golden shore.

Two years ago to-morrow—
    How long to me they seem!
My girl and I were wooing
    Beside this very stream!

Her humid eyes, so dreamy,
    Made shame the stars above,—
While her voice so sweet and mellow,
    Was like the voice of Love!

But now she sweetly slumbers
    Beneath the dewy sod,
While wings her angel spirit
    Around the throne of God!

To My Wife

At Kingston, Jamaica, West Indies

THOU art gone to thine island home,
    On the Caribbean shore—
Gone to thy dear old native scenes,
    Among thy friends of yore.

May health, and joy, and hope be thine,
    Dear comfort of my life;
May Heaven's protecting care attend
    My darlings and my wife!

Two little darlings, sweet and bright,
    With tiny hands and feet—
With raven hair and jetty eyes,
    And voices dear and sweet.

They are my jewels and my wealth—
    My joy, my life, my all;
And heavenly music 'tis to me
    Whene'er I hear them call!

But they are gone, and I, alone,
    Am lonesome and bereft;
My life has been a joyless blank
    E'er since my darlings left.

But, ah! this sadd'ning loneliness
    Will last for but a time:
They'll soon return, and, in my heart,
    I'll hear their voices chime!

My darling wife and little ones,
　　Far o'er the foaming main,
Weeks will be months, and months long years,
　　Until you come again!

———

COME back to me, come back to me,
From o'er the foaming, raging sea:
Come back—your home is in my heart,
And from its fold no more depart.

Come back, for days and nights are drear,
And home seems desolate and queer;
The sunny joys of home have fled,
And chaos reigns o'er floor and bed.

Come back, your chickens go half-fed;
The weeds have worn—your flow'rs are dead!
Disorder rules supreme o'er all,
And webs are thick on every wall.

Come back with sunny joys and smiles,
Come back with laughing hearts and eyes;
Come back to soothe, come back to cheer,
And all this sad confusion clear.

To Madame Selika

O SIREN of the colored race,
   With matchless voice and queenly grace!
'Tis thine to move the heart to tears,
   And lift it to the upper spheres!

Sweet heavenly gifts to thee belong,
   To heal our ills with magic song;
And make our drooping hearts rejoice
   With the sweet pathos of thy voice!

Enchantress from the sunset glow!
   Thy notes in mellow cadence flow;
Like music from a hidden lyre,
   Or echoes from the heavenly choir!

Selika! thou art sent to shame,
   The scoffers of our race, who blame,
And curse the Negro for his skin,—
   And wrong him for this God-sent sin!

On the Banks of the St. Johns

MAJESTIC stream! vast inland sea!
   Great mirror of the skies;
Upon thy banks I'll sing of thee,
   While thy tides fall and rise!

Thy bosom, stretching far away,
   Into the woodland green:
Now turbid, angry surges sway—
   Now lulled in sweet serene!

Thy grandeur now inspires my heart
   With sentiments sublime;
And while I muse my thoughts depart
   Upon thy waves' sweet chime!

I sit enraptured, and am bound
   With feelings strange and sweet:
Enchantment burdens every sound
   Which the charmed waves repeat.

Far, far away on rippling waves,
   Sweet heavenly grandeurs ride;
The golden sunshine sports and laves
   Upon thy rolling tide!

Majestic stream, thy beauty feeds
   The senses with delight,
And from its gloomy portal leads
   The heart to heavenly light.

Sweet heavenly vision!—fairy stream
   For which the poets long,
O, could I put thy beauty's gleam
   Into immortal song!

This sweet enchantment and the spell
   That binds me to thy shore,
Will live in memory's secret cell,
   A charm forevermore.

And now farewell majestic stream!—
   Ye sun kissed waves in strife:
Your grandeur will forever seem
   The day-dream of my life!

Homeward Bound

SPREAD her snowy riggings wide,
Turn her prow towards the tide;
Let the sailor's song resound,
As we o'er the breakers bound!

Steer her to my native hills,
To my valleys, streams and rills,
Steer her to my own dear shore,
To the lov'd ones home once more.

Hear the sailors' voices sound,
As we merrily, merrily bound,
O'er the angry ocean's foam,
As we plow towards my home!

Joyous hearts and sparkling eyes,
Wait us 'neath our own blue skies,
Waiting for our souls to cheer,
With a happy, welcome tear!

Soon upon my natal shore,
There to greet kind friends once more,
Sweet will be the kiss I ween,
Of my maiden love and *queen!*

Perhaps You'd Like to Know

I HAVE a gentle love, whose eyes,
  With softest radiance glow;
She is a seraph from the skies
  To cheer me here below!

Her mellow voice fills me with bliss,
  With its soft silvery flow:
And who this angel being is,
  Perhaps you'd like to know!

I won this dark-eyed maiden in
  Sweet hours of long ago;
And how her heart I chanced to win,
  Perhaps you'd like to know.

She is a gentle fairy queen—
  With pearly teeth of snow;
The arms that press this maid, I ween,
  You'd really like to know!

My thoughts, like swift, unfettered creeks,
  To this sweet angel flow;
The lips that kiss her crimson cheeks
  Perhaps you'd like to know!

It is this fairy one that gives
  Me hope and joy below:
And where this little creature lives,
  Perhaps you'd like to know!

My Sister

SHE has pass'd from our band like a heavenly vision,
    The simple, the kind gentle hearted,
They have lain her so gently, so sweetly to slumber,
    In her tomb among the departed.

She has pass'd from our number, and we mourn her so sadly,
    Her mother, her father and brother,
We mourn her so deeply, so greatly and meekly
    Because we have not another.

On her grave in the garden, her mother has planted,
    Sweet jessamines, lilies and roses,
While beneath their perfumery her pure angel spirit,
    So calmly and sweetly reposes.

Sweet Josephine, rest, in thy mansion above!
    From turmoil, temptation and sorrow;
Thy pure spirit now, with the angels is winging,
    And fears not the cares of the morrow!

Music

SWEET Music throws her arms
   Around the weary heart,
And with her mystic charms,
   Bids its rude cares depart.

Like incense sweet it falls,
   Upon the din-worn ear:
And with her voice she calls
   The soul from heavy fear,—

Like odor sweet it floats,
   Upon the midnight air,
Like angels' softest notes,
   From the celestial choir!

Sweet Music—gift of Heaven!
   Disperser of our wo,
To thee is power given,
   To cheer us here below.

We hear thy voice below—
   We hear it sound above;
Which sets our hearts aglow
   With life, and joy, and love.

We Are Parted Now Forever

WE are parted now forever,
  Though our hearts were truly one;
Every plighted vow is broken,
  Every beam of love is gone.

Gentle, pure, unstained—go mingle
  In the world's gay, festive throng;
Let no sad, unbidden memory
  Cause thy simple heart to long.

Thickly fall the shades of sorrow
  Round my sad heart's altar now;
While a silent secret passion
  Rages over mind and brow.

Though life's guiding star seems hidden
  By this brooding, lowering gloom,
Yet upon this waste, now barren,
  Hope's fair flowers yet may bloom.

We are parted—sadly parted,
  But perhaps 'tis not for life;
Love's sweet memory may yet conquer
  Passion's hot and fleeting strife.

Charles Sumner

A MONUMENt of prayer and thanks—
   A monument of tears!
Is all that we can offer thee,
   Dear friend of many years.

No towering bronze or marble,
   To mark thy resting place;
Thy lasting monument shall be,
   THE FREEDOM OF OUR RACE!

Our hopes have almost follow'd thee
   Into the silent grave;
For thou wert our tower of strength
   When man made man a slave.

The blow of Brooks upon thy head,
   Shine forth like diadems,
And the bondman's broken fetters,
   Are thy crown's richest gems.

The nation has lost a pillar,
   And we, a bosom friend:
Who can e'er with equal power
   Our Civil Rights defend?

Thou art passed from earth, O, Sumner!
   Leaving thy work undone;
May He who called thee off, complete
   Thy work so well begun.

We must not faint by the wayside,
    But hope and trust and pray;
Our journey leads from dark to light—
    To Freedom's perfect day.

To General Grant

AN ACROSTIC

GREAT chief of war—no less renowned in peace,
Enter again upon thy second lease.
Never give ear to slanders; do the part
Entrusted to thee by the Nation's heart
Rightly, humbly, as best to thee may seem,
And then is yours the people's deep esteem.
Lead on again, Columbia's chosen son,
Great peer of "Father Abe" and Washington!
Rally again the sovereigns of the soil,
Ah! not to war, but to the fruits of toil.
No North or South, no section far or near;
The PEOPLE, *all*, demand thy equal care.

A Retrospect

TO-NIGHT my pensive thoughts are cast
Far down the cloud-land of the Past,
Amid the scenes when life appeared
Bright, new and young, and more endeared—
More free from cares and burning tears
Than ever since in after years.

O, memories of the long ago!
When will you tire and cease to flow,
And stay in your dim vaults confined,
Beyond the portals of my mind?
But no! I would not have you cease
Your messages of love and peace;
Sweet dreams and consolation bring
Forever on your viewless wing!

Our gentle loves are with the Past,
They are too pure and good to last;
How dear the echo of their feet,
And prattling, music voices sweet,
Resounding from the faded shore,
Of the bright realm of golden yore!
Through the dim space of by-gone years,
Some little darling's face appears;
A rosy pledge of wedded love,
Returned to its bright fold above.

The Past to us seems ever dear—
The Future full of gloom and fear:
The one we know its where and when—
The other is beyond our ken.

Youth is allied to joy and life;
Age to sorrow, care, and strife:
The one is like the fount that flows—
The other, winter, with its snows!
Such are Life's lessons—such the ends
To which our groveling nature tends,
Till gathered, when the Reaper comes,
Into our destined, unknown homes.

To My Love

COME to me my fairy queen,
  To these waiting arms;
Thou'rt lovely, and I mean
  To extol thy charms.

Dimpled hands, jetty eyes,
  Locks of raven hue;
Sweet bosom, full of sighs,
  Tender, warm and true.

Glowing cheeks, dimpled chin,
  Silken lashes long;
Rosy lips, soft and thin,
  Portals of sweet song!

Sweet charms, for ever dear—
  Dear as dear can be;
They are mine; love, come near,
  You belong to me!

Now through the cares of life,
  Constant, true and strong;
Be my joy, and my wife,
  Though the way be long!

A Peace Offering

Suggested by Lamar's speech on Sumner

HAIL spirit of triumphant Peace!
  Come down in bright attire
Like Minerva 'mid the arms of Greece
  To quell Achilles' ire.

'Tis time, O North and South, to cease
  These hates and strifes of yore,
And turn into the paths of peace
  Like brothers now, once more.

Be brothers now forever hence,
  In mutual love and toil;
Go forth with manly confidence—
  Twin monarchs of the soil!

No North, no South, no East, no West,
  One country, flag and God:
The passions of the past should rest
  With heroes 'neath the sod.

We are one people, with one aim,
  One destiny, one cause—
Striving for greatness, power and fame,
  With equal rank and laws.

Arise and cease to sorrow o'er
  The fortunes of the past;
They're gone: our hopes must be for more
  In the bright future cast.

Is It Worth While?

Is IT worth while in these shadowy vales
  To build on Hope's delusive wing?
They are the soul's prison: its sighs and wails
  Are winters where succeeds a spring!

Life blooms and fades; but there's more dark than light,
  If we the inner shadows take:
Our transitory joys and fleet delight
  Are oases in life's sandy wake.

Is it worth while for us to sorrow o'er
  The fearful horrors of the grave?
Our parted ones, far on the Unknown Shore,
  For earthly joys no longer crave.

Is it worth while to build with misspent years
  A fleeting paradise below?
Our joys are brief at best, bedimmed with tears,
  And marred with gnawing, untold woe.

The sunshine of the heart lingers not long,
  But yields to life's dark inner clouds,
That float incessantly in boding throng,
  Like gloomy Death's appalling shrouds!

This life is brief at best; sow goodly seed
  Of lasting joys beyond the tomb!
O, sweet harvest joys —Love's true labor's meed,
  That in Elysium forever bloom!

Easter Hymn

HALLELUJAH! Christ has risen!
From the tomb's cold, gloomy prison!
And to fallen man has given
Hope of endless joys in heaven!

He has risen in His glory,
Mary, go and tell the story,
To His chosen, faithful leaders,
Who are for His Kingdom pleaders.

See! the glory of the morning,
Judah's hills and vales adorning,
With a splendor, bright and glowing—
With the rays of glory flowing!

Hallelujah! Christ has risen!
From the powers of the prison,
To His Father's shining glory,
Go and tell the joyful story!

Speak to Me Kindly

O SPEAK to me kindly,
  Harsh words have no power;
They touch not the heart
  In its sorrowing hour.

Kind words fitly spoken
  Reach down to the heart;
And with secret power
  Bid its sorrows depart.

O, speak kindly ever,
  In sunshine or storm;
It will soften rude cares,
  And keep the heart warm.

Then speak to me kindly
  Dear friend of my heart;
And from thy sweet presence
  I'll never depart!

My Talisman

My talisman reposes
 Amid shrubbery green,
And sweet summer roses
 Of white and crimson sheen.

Where sunbeams are wooing
 The flower and the vine,
And plaintive doves cooing,
 On boughs of oak and pine.

Dear spot where I'm "farming" —
 "My small world set apart,"
A goal forever charming,
 Unto my eyes and heart!

Home is not home never,
 Unless its joys and charms,
Cheer one's memory ever,
 Through life's dark, beating storms.

Four little eyes beaming
 With love and hope complete—
Four little hands seeming,
 To vie with restless feet!

Two little heads dozing,
 Dreaming of fairy things—
Like angels reposing,
 In bed with folded wings!

Cup of earthly pleasure
 Brimful of rosy joy;
Holding all my treasure—
 My bright-eyed girl and boy!

To L.E.M.

I WANT an ideal—a Platonic friend,
  To whom I humbly could address
The passions of my muse, and not offend,
  But with sweet joy her heart impress.

I've scann'd thy features well, and mark'd thy eyes,
  And sat enraptured with thy voice;
Sipping its music with deep drawn sighs,
  Until I felt my heart rejoice!

Thou art *my ideal!* wilt thou heed my strain,
  And be the goddess of my mind?
Sweet will be the task: thou shalt not complain,
  But soar *above* all womankind!

If thou consent, O then, thy heart prepare
  For missives of the poet's art;
I'll sing of love and dreams, and beauty rare,
  And storm the portals of thy heart!

To the Same

O, PLEAD not inability to cope
    With my poor, simple muse;
Thou has the latent germ and hope,
    If thou but effort use.

The golden ore in Western lands,
    Is hidden in the mine;
Till summoned forth by patient hands,
    To conquer and to shine!

I've seen the germ deep down thy eyes,
    Just like the hidden ore;
And patient effort will suffice
    To make its lustre sure.

My patient pen and heart, and mind,
    Shall seek this precious ore;
Until like fashioned gold refined,
    It shines forth bright and pure!

I know not why my poor muse wings
    Her jealous way to thee:
And with impatience, ever sings
    Thy praises unto me.

Thou art not beautiful, and yet,
    There is a grace divine,
Serenely sweet, and deeply set
    In that fair face of thine.

Thanks for thy friendship and thy praise,
    I'll prize them evermore;
They'll cheer me through long, weary days,
    When other joys are o'er.

A Love Song

My love has gone to roam,
  Beyond the deep blue sea;
But my kisses on his cheek
  Will bring him back to me.

Although he is away,
  Far on a distant shore;
He left his heart behind,
  With me forevermore!

I feel the lingering glow
  Of his kisses even now;
Like sunny beams of morn
  Upon my cheek and brow!

Dear darling of my heart—
  Star of my blooming life;
I've vow'd, on your return,
  To be your darling wife!

The Murdered Bride

FAR away in Balize there lived
   A Spanish-Indian maid;
And fair was she to look upon,
   Her name was Adelaide.

Coyish, and beautiful and meek,
   She was fair nature's child;
Her eyes were black, her flowing hair
   Made her look strange and wild.

But sadness dwelt upon her heart,
   Her mother long had died; —
Her father led a hostile band,
   And the fierce arrow plied.

Her life was sad, and yet at times,
   Hope brightened all her heart;
And she would bid the silent woe
   From her poor heart depart.

She loved a fair, young Englishman,
   Who roam'd upon the sea;
And when he wrote her month by month,
   Her heart was full of glee.

What dreams had she of blissful years
   Of rosy, wedded life!
In twelve more moons, she was to be
   A happy bride and wife!

How fair is life when love and hope,
    Together rule the heart;
How fleet upon their fairy wings,
    Our thoughts to heaven start!

But there are tears, and nights, and storms
    In life, as well as light;
The heart that beams with joy to-day,
    To-morrow's storms may blight.

Poor Adelaide! fair child of woe!
    Thy father long had sworn,
That thy young pale-face lover should
    Ne'er take thee for his own!

The twelve moons pass'd; poor Adelaide,
    Her heart with true love burned,
For on a fair and hopeful day,
    The Englishman returned.

Her black eyes gleamed with hope and joy,
    She felt her heart rejoice;
For months and years had come and gone,
    Since she had heard his voice.

That night at the small village church,
    The priest had joined their hands;
And they were bound, in two more days,
    To sail for other lands.

But ere they reached their bridal home,
    That night, poor Adelaide,
A ghastly, bloody, bridal corpse,
    Was by her father made!

In Mama's Bed

EVERY morning she comes creeping,
   Little Mamie in her gown,
From her little bed half sleeping,
   With her dreamy eyes cast down.

"Mama, I am cold, please let me
   Come and sleep into your bed."
And, getting in, quite bold and free,
   Covers up her little head.

Mama, with mock surprise out-cries—
   "What big girl is this, I pray,
Who from her bed before sun rise,
   Gets up at the break of day?"

And Mamie laughs, and creeping near,
   Gives mama the morning kiss!
Now who can in this mortal sphere
   Measure this eternal bliss?

O Father, at the final morn,
   Let my Mamie sleep with Thee!
Let this sweet darling—my last born,
   In Thy courts an angel be!

Parted

WE'RE parted now, and far apart we dwell,
   On the cold borders of this vale of tears,
Yet oftentimes in a sweet dreamy spell,
   Your gentle form before my sight appears,

With all the beauty and the power of grace,
   That once unmanned me in the bygone days;
With the same eyes and happy sunlit face
   That won my love, my life, my sweetest praise!

But soon is fled this mystic, dreamy spell,
   When memory opes her magic folding door;
Again my thoughts on worldly misery dwell—
   Again I tread the desert as before.

I steady walk life's rugged road alone,
   And try to drive thy image from my mind,
With the sweet memories of days by-gone,
   That still my heart and tender feelings bind!

A Visit to My Native Home

O, HOW I love to linger near,
  These scenes and ties of yore!
They call up mem'ries sweet and dear
  To me forevermore!

Here is the rustic house of logs,
  Hewn broad with axe and line;
And steers, and cows, and mules, and dogs,
  And restless, nosing swine!

And down below the cotton wood,
  The dear old river sweeps;
While on its bank in solitude
  The flowing willow weeps.

How oft upon its rippling wave
  I've swept with splashing oars,
And gliding down, to fish and lave,
  Upon its pebbled shores!

And yonder waves the golden field
  Of ripening wheat and corn;
What cheerful hopes upon its yield
  And worth are daily born!

Farewell, sweet native home again—
  Scenes of my boyhood's plays!
Your ties and memories will remain
  The bright dream of my days!

Free Cuba

HAIL free Cuba! Queen of the tropic sea,
Thy long bound, toil-worn, sable sons are free!
The fiat has gone forth, from sea to sea,
That men, no longer slaves, but free shall be!
It is the voice of Freedom's patient God,
That man shall groan no more beneath the rod!
The Cuban slaves have heard the swelling sound
Of Freedom's hosts fast marching on the ground,
Where late through fire and blood, with sword and gun,
The glorious war for Liberty was won!
March onward, glorious band, for equal rights,
God makes man free when he for freedom fights!
Cowards are always slaves, and have no share,
In the sweet spoils of those who *do* and *dare*!
Cuba is free! now let Brazil awake,
From her vile bondage, and her fetters break!
And join the northern chorus of the free,
That swells from land to land and sea to sea!

Under the Pine and Palm

FAR from the city's din and strife,
And from the scenes of busy life,

I wander to the woodland bow'rs
Where I may muse through the pensive hours.

Under the pine, under the palm,
In sombre shadows soft and calm;

The atmosphere, though charged with heat,
Is filled with woodland odors sweet.

Up in the boughs of verdant trees,
Where sports the gentle fleetful breeze,

The merry birds, with tiny throats,
Chirp out their songs in sweetest notes.

Fair Nature in her best array,
Sits crowned, the floral Queen of May;

The sunbeams on the vine-clad bow'rs,
Descend in gentle, golden show'rs.

Sweet May! forever fair and bright—
For e'er ladened with sweet delight!—

'Tis thine to cheer our lonely hours,
And deck this sunny land with flow'rs.

Sweet summer land, forever green,
With climate blissful and serene;

No icy wind with chilling snows,
Around thy fairy borders blows.

O, arching pines with towering height,
Grim watchers of the silent night!—

Have ye no tales of wild romance
To lure my soul in blissful trance?

Perhaps beneath these very bow'rs,
In by-gone happy days and hours,

The warrior and the Indian maid,
Sweet vows of lasting love have made.

How pure and simple in the woods,
Is love in all its varied moods:

Its life, an endless summer day,
With no dark clouds to foil its sway.

But I must leave these sunny bow'rs,
With their enchanted birds and flow'rs:

These are but tastes to mortals given,
Of that endless Spring in Heaven!

Absence

O WHAT a dreary blank! how long
   These dragging months have been
Since thou wert here with cheerful song,
   And with thy smile serene!

Thy presence was my life, my joy—
   Thy voice was my delight,
And how must I the time employ
   When thou art out of sight?

I sigh in sadness all alone,
   In daytime and at eve;
From out my heart the light is gone,
   And I in sorrow grieve.

I sit, then walk from place to place,
   And dream of thee at night;
And in my wearied mind I trace
   Thy features sweet and bright!

O darling, come to me again!
   And cheer my heart once more,—
Come in thy beauty and remain,
   And joy and life restore!

Frederick Douglass

FROM servile state to highest fame,
This Nestor of the black race came.

What a change, and wonderful span,
For a fettered and slave-cursed man!

Some call us an "inferior race,"
And to the ape our lineage trace;

But what man of a fairer hue
Could ever this black man out-do?

All honor to this Negro sage,
Who on the Anti-Slavery stage,

With other leaders of its foes,
Dealt Slavery such deadly blows!

Rejoice! For now at last behold,
Thy race no longer bought and sold!

Rest from thy work, and with joy see,
Four millions of thy people free!

"So Near and Yet So Far"

"THOU art so far and yet so near,"
  By day and night to me;
I've seen thee only twice this year,
  Although firm friends are we.

And yet deep in thy woman's heart
  A chamber clean and pure
To me is sacred; kept apart
  For our tried love of yore.

O sacred chamber, Cupid's shrine,
  Art thou forever sealed?
And shall those treasured gems of thine
  Be never more revealed?

Ah, words were vain; our hearts and eyes
  A silent language knew;
When thou, confused with tears and sighs,
  I to my bosom drew!

My lips again may never press
  The hot tears on thy face;
Nor I thy slender form caress
  In one long, fond embrace!

Such luxuries of love belong
  Unto the faded past;
But still for these dear sweets I long,
  E'en though apart we're cast.

Then be not far when thou art near,
  But near my heart abide;
There dream and hope, and do not fear,
  Although dark years betide!

The Negro's Lament

HOW LONG, O God! how long must I remain
    Worse than an alien in my native land?
For long years past I've toiled for other's gain
    Beneath Oppression's ruthless iron hand.

Columbia! why art thou so great and fair,
    And so false and cruel to thine own?
Goodness and Beauty, a proverbial pair,
    They in thy heritage, themselves disown.

So fair and yet so false! thou art a lie
    Against both natural and human laws,—
A deformed dwarf, dropp'd from an angry sky
    To serve a selfish and unholy cause!

Ye sun-kiss'd lakes and hills of Liberty!
    And silvery flowing streams and fields!
Your teeming gold and grain are not for me,
    My birthright only ostracism yields!

My life is burdensome; year succeeds year
    With feeble hope: I try to emulate
All that conspire to ennoble manhood's sphere;
    And yet I seem to war with angry Fate!

O Liberty! I taste but half thy sweets
    In this thy boasted land of Equal Rights!
Although I've fought on land and in thy fleets
    Thy foes, by day and by dim camp-fire lights!

What more wouldst have me do? Is not my life—
    My blood, an all-sufficient sacrifice?
Wouldst thou have me transformed in the vain strife
    To change the fiat of the great Allwise?

Of what avail is life—why sigh and fret,
    When manly hopes are only born to fade?
Although declared a man, a vassal yet
    By social caste—a crime by heaven made!

Far better for me not to have been born,
    Than live and feel the frownings of mankind;
Endure its social hatred and its scorn,
    With all my blighting, forlorn hopes combined.

O, cruel fate!—O, struggle which unmans,
    And burdens every hope and every sigh!
Thou art a boundless gulf over which spans
    Only the arching, storm-foreboding sky!

Ah, woe is me! I feel my yearnings crush'd
    Ere they are born within my sighing heart;
All hopes, all manly aspirations hush'd
    As with the power of Death's fatal dart!

The rice birds sing as if in mocking glee,
    Scorn my long felt sorrows and my burning tears,
Why mock me, birds? I only crave to be
    Like you, free to roam the boundless spheres!

But still sing on! your cheerful music gives
    My fading hope a gleam of brighter days;
Why should I grieve? the eternal God still lives!—
    The sun still shines though clouds obscure his rays!

The darkest hour is just before the break
    Of dawning victory of light and life,
When Freedom's hosts with armor bright awake,
    To quell Oppression in the deadly strife!

New hope is mine! for now I see the gleam
    Of beacon lights of coming liberty!
A continent is shock'd—a crimson stream
    Of blood has paid the debt, and I am free!

To E.W.S.

THOU art divinely tall and fair,
And crowned with auburn, flaxen hair;
A charming shape to thee was given
By the presiding Fates of heaven!
That witching mole upon thy cheek,
Renders thy features sweet and meek;
It is a witching charm and pet,
That is in thy pale beauty set.
That beauty from the southern clime,
Beams on thy face with love sublime,—
A southern jessamine thou art,
For thou has won my trusting heart!
O could I win that heart of thine,
And call it hence forever mine!
I'd count my earthly sorrows o'er,
And dream of bliss forever more!

A Sonnet

THE SUN, upon the western sky,
   Has painted ev'ry cloud with gold;
And now he shuts his fiery eye
   To sleep in his hesperian fold!
And twilight with presumptuous Night,
   Are battling on the plain for sway;
While in the dell, in sweet delight,
   The nightingale pipes out his lay.
The new-born Moon, with silver sheen,
   Now seeks the gloomy earth to woo;
While from the Stars, glad tears are seen
   To fall in crystal drops of dew,
Into the cups of gay-eyed flow'rs,
   That sparkle bright from woodland bow'rs!

The Erring

Down from the height of virtue's throne—
   Out on the world's cold sea!
She glides, a sad, forsaken one,
   Once happy, proud and free.
Love was her sin; too strong and well
   That passion swayed her heart;
Its power ruled her life—she fell
   A victim to its dart.

If "God is love" can love be sin
   On earth more than in Heaven?
That flame that burned her heart within
   Was by her Saviour given.
"She loved not wisely, but too well,"
   So says the world of pride;
And with its scorn her sighs would quell,
   And her poor life deride.

The Cross was for the fallen made—
   For these the Saviour died;
And why heap burdens—why upbraid
   Their lives with mocking pride?
Their lot is sad enough. No more
   Their darkened lives defame;
Better to bid their sorrows o'er
   Than sink their hearts in shame.

A gentle look—a tender word,
    May cheer the erring maid;
And touch a secret, silent chord
    Of hope that may not fade.
In solitude she sits alone,
    Wrapped up in grief and woe;
The sunshine of her life is gone,
    Her lover too, also.

Deep gloom is locked within her soul,
    Her eyes are filled with tears;
She sees the clouds of sorrow roll
    Over her future years.
She hates herself the worst of all,
    Her love is still the same
For him who brought her to her fall,
    And made her life a shame.

Kind Father of the high and low—
    The fallen and the good;
Look kindly on this child of woe
    In her dark solitude!
Bring back the sunshine of her life,
    And once more make her bloom,
That she may be a spirit wife
    Beyond the silent tomb!

The Return

I AM come again to my native land!
   From the far off bounding sea—
Once more to my own dear hills and dales,
   With a spirit light and free!

Once more to my native scenes and skies—
   Once more to the loved ones home:
Once more to my placid streams and lakes,
   I merrily, merrily come!

Once more 'mid the din and clash of swords—
   'Mid the roar of musketry!
Where the daring sable warrior strikes
   For GOD and LIBERTY!

Once more 'mid the flow of blood and tears—
   Where the cannon's iron voice,
Speaks Freedom on the Southern plains,
   And makes the slave rejoice!

Once more to my dark-eyed maiden-love,
   To make her red cheeks glow!
Once more to the angel heart I won
   In days of long ago!

In Memoriam

Died.—At Tallahassee, Fla., February 11, 1875,
for want of thirty-nine votes, a band of patriots named Legion

OH who in story or in song
Can tell the pangs of those who long
For envied senatorial fame,
Without the *votes* to get the same?
What pen can write and language tell
The sighs and woes of those who fell
Prostrate and bleeding in the race,
With "U.S.S." stamped in their face?

Ah, "thirty-nine," immortal prize!
That dazzled patriotic eyes;
For thee they struggled, prayed and sighed,
For thee they fought and lost and died!

Take them up—no; let them repose,
Peacefully from their crushing woes;
Let their friends send off the story
That they died in *sight* of glory!

"Well, such is life:" to-day we bloom,
To—morrow we are wrapped in gloom:
Now you have it—it looks so fine—
Now you don't, 'twas all moonshine!

Centennial Hymn

O SILENT harp! awake and greet
   Freedom's Centennial morn,
With thrilling numbers soft and sweet
   And melodies new born!

Safe from despotic thrones we sing
   Sweet anthems of the free;
We pray in peace, and fear no King
   Beyond the surging sea!

Thank God for Puritanical zeal,
   On freedom's virgin sod,
That bravely sought, in woe or weal,
   "Freedom to worship God!"

Thanks for the faith that would not yield,
   Nor shrink at death's alarm;
God was its hope and prayer and shield,
   And truth its secret charm!

Calmly beneath the western skies,
   Young freedom sighs no more;
For he is stout and loud defies
   The tyrant's rule of yore!

On every hill—on every plain,
   His rustic throne is seen;
The yeoman form his regal train—
   The milkmaid is his queen!

Equality of rights and laws—
   Equality of birth;
These are the glories of our cause,
   The treasures of our worth.

These are the golden fruits enjoyed—
   A century's first yield:
From patient, rugged hands employed
   In freedom's martial field!

O let these ties unite again,
   Our sections near and far;
And gently lure them to refrain
   From the dread work of war.

Then tuneful harp, with pride repeat
   The dear Centennial joy;
With thrilling numbers soft and sweet,
   Thy highest notes employ!

On the Death of Wm. Lloyd Garrison

At last thy sword is sheathed, O Garrison!
  Brave warrior for the trampled Right!
Though dead, thy voice is ever marching on
  Where Right is fettered under Might!

Mellow with age, with honors laden bright,
  Thou hast pass'd from the world's great strife:
Through the wrongs and crimes of Oppression's night,
  To the gates of a peaceful life!

To-day five million hearts in sorrow grieve—
  Five million voices sing thy praise;
For with thy sword their fetters thou didst cleave,
  And numbered Slavery's bloody days!

To-day let Liberty's fair face be bowed,
  And let her banners bright be furled;
For her brave giant in his grave is lowered,
  Who braved the darts that slavery hurled!

Thy work on earth, O Garrison, was done,
  Like righteous Simeon of old;
Thy eyes did see our Freedom's battle won,
  And Man no longer bought and sold!

All honor to thy name, O Garrison!
  And the brave ones who with thee fought,—
Forten, Purvis, Tappan, and bold Thompson,
  Phillips, Douglass, Lucretia Mott!

Thou art gone to thy rest, no more to flee,
  From a vile Philadelphia mob:
No more to plead for the slave to be free
  From those who his labor did rob!

The slave is free! thou didst not plead in vain!
  For God is ever with the Right;
And those who trade in human souls for gain,
  Are doomed to fall below His might!

Rest from thy labors in thy honoured grave,
  While prayers ascend to Freedom's God;
His glory has been seen, and now the slave
  No longer groans beneath the rod!

I Dare Not Tell Thee

I DARE not tell thee how thy stately form
    Sweeps with majestic grace;
Divinely beautiful, with magic charm,
    Before my pensive face.

I dare not tell thee how thy modest eyes,
    Illume my inmost heart;
And draw from it such secret, hopeless sighs,
    As make its fibers smart.

I dare not tell thee all I think and feel,
    Nor all I dream of thee;
All this is sacred; nor must I reveal
    How dear thou art to me!

I dare not tell thee how I crave to be
    Thy chosen, favored friend;
To share thy great, warm heart, so large and free,
    Its thoughts to comprehend!

To rule supreme o'er such a heart as thine,
    And call thee "darling wife!"
What king or poet who would not enshrine
    Thee in his heart for life!

Such thoughts and dreams as these alone belong
    Unto a poet's mind;
To be rehearsed in his impassioned song,
    Of love and womankind!

There is enthroned high on thy queenly brow,
   A charm divinely sweet;
Before whose power *man* must ever bow
   In homage at thy feet!

My heart is prisoned; I must say no more
   Until thy smile I greet,
I pray thee do not chide my muse before
   We at the church-door meet!

Autumn

A GLIMMERING haze upon the landscape rests;
The sky has a softer robe of blue;
And the slant sunbeams glisten mildly through
The floating clouds, that light their pearly crests
Mid the pure currents of the upper air.
The fields are dressed in Autumn's faded green,
And trees no more their clustering foliage wear;
Yet Nature smiles, all lovely and serene.
How sweetly breaths this life-inspiring gale,
Stirring broad Potomac's transparent wave;
Could I but dream that Winter, cold and pale,
Might never o'er this scene of beauty rave,
Or touch the waters with his icy spear,—
O, would these golden hours be half so dear?

The Solid South

THE monster, Treason, still survives!
   And in the South domain,
The Negroes, trembling for their lives,
   For justice plead in vain!

How long, O God of truth, how long,
   Shall those vile gangs abound,
And with their guns, in numbers strong,
   Shoot Negroes to the ground?

All o'er the South's fair sunny clime,
   Is heard the rebel yell,
Where through the war, in manly prime,
   The Union soldier fell.

The North was fooled, too soon the strife
   Was closed, and pardon given,
To those who on the Nation's life
   In bloody war had striven.

But see! the solid North arrayed
   In glory and in might;
And like a giant, undismayed,
   Again renews the fight!

It thunders from the Northern lakes—
   It is the voice of God!
The giant tramp of Freedom shakes
   The loyal Northern sod!

Let Treason and its hordes beware,
   Lest Freedom's hosts again,
With sword, and shot, and shell, lay bare
   Its unsubdued domain!

To a Lady Friend

FAIR lady, minstrel of the heart,
  With regal, winsome ways
And fairy fingers that impart
  The power of magic lays,

'Tis thine with tender notes to stir
  The heart's most secret spring,
And be its soft interpreter,
  And all its yearnings sing.

'Tis thine to touch with magic hands,
  The keys of sweet delight,
And waft the soul to fairy lands,
  In heavenly regions bright.

A power divine belongs to thee
  To please and melt the heart,
And bid with potent melody
  All its rude cares depart!

In silent joy my soul once fed
  Upon thy numbers sweet;
Their charm, though weary days have fled,
  Still holds my heart complete.

Good-Bye! Off for Kansas

GOOD-BYE ye bloody scenes of long ago!—
  Good-bye to cotton fields and hounds!
From you, vile sources of my earthly woe,
  My freed and leaping spirit bounds!

Though free, my work to me no profit yields,
  And for my politics, am mobb'd;
No more thank God! upon these bloody fields
  Shall I be of my labor robb'd!

Good-bye Aunt Polly! good-bye Uncle Ned!
  I am off, and shall not come back;
This land is cursed; we are in rags, half fed,
  Bull-dosed and killed by Yellow Jack!

Good-bye! I've sold my little cane and corn!
  And am off for the river's banks;
And when I step on board to-morrow morn,
  I'll sing and give the good Lord thanks!

To Lucy

Lucy, push your veil aside,
  When you pass my store;
Let me see those eyes you hide,
  Then I'll love you more!

Dreamy eyes and chubby face,
  Let me see you more;
Full of love and life and grace!
  When you pass my store!

How I watch to see you pass,
  With your graceful mien;
Gliding like a young school lass
  Of joyous seventeen!

If you love me not, then why
  Do you pass this way?
Don't you know you make me sigh
  With your form so gay?

Lines Written in "Pet's" Album

O, MARY, you have ruled too long
   O'er prostrate bleeding hearts;
Lay by your scepter; why prolong
   Your sway with Cupid's darts?

Brave Hymen with extended arms
   Your long delay upbraids;
Yield to his care your queenly charms
   Before your beauty fades!

Our District School Teachers

WHAT shall I write or say,
    About this noble band,
Who toil from day to day,
    With eyes, and heart, and hand?

The care and toil and woes,
    From morn till coming eve,
A teacher undergoes,
    No one else can conceive.

A noisy mob of brats,
    One good to twenty bad,
With toys and strings and hats,
    Enough to send one mad!

The teacher's hell is here—
    Their heaven is above
The *whispering* atmosphere,
    Through which they daily move!

And yet with all this care,
    They still are bright and *sane*—
They smile at grim despair,
    And their good looks retain!

God bless you one and all!
    And may the day soon come,
When Cupid's voice should call
    You all to Hymen's home!

Acrostic

MAJESTIC one! with regal form and mien,
A modern type thou art of Egypt's queen:
Robust and tall, and crowned with raven hair,
You are my ideal of a woman fair!

For many years thy form has seem'd to me
Replete with beauty and nobility:
Awakening hopes and dreams, only to fade
'Neath the dark wing of Fate's desponding shade.
Cannot some pleasant memories of yore
Enter thy heart and thoughts of me restore?
Send them not back, they are in friendship made!

Kindle anew the friendship of the past,
If in thy heart a spark of it be left;
Grant me this boon, its memory will last
Evermore undimm'd, till I of life be reft,
Respond to father Gabriel's final blast!

Phillis Wheatley

FROM out the gloom and shade of years—
   From out the vault of time;
O, Phillis, fill these lowly spheres
   With thy sweet notes sublime!

Thy silent harp, O strike again,
   Upon the Unknown Shore,
That I may catch the sweet refrain
   And sing thy numbers o'er!

Celestial fire to thee was given
   To move the heart to tears,
And lull, with melting notes of heaven,
   Its yearnings and its fears!

Too soon thy tuneful harp was hush'd
   By death's relentless dart;
To soon thy fairy hopes were crush'd
   Within thy singing heart.

Dear Phillis, let me write thy name
   Into immortal song;
So that thy worth and glowing fame
   May be remembered long.

I've never seen thy pensive face,
   Nor heard thy cheerful voice;
And yet through Fancy's dream I trace
   The Muse's sable choice.

I love the sweetness of thy song,
   And hold thy memory dear;
Thy genius and thy fame belong
   To Negroes far and near.

To M.E.T.

ACROSTIC

My dear, new friend, with features fair,
And sparkling eyes and waving hair,
Rude care has not yet touched thy face,
To mar its sweetness and its grace.
He was a fool to turn his heart
Against such creatures as thou art!

Thy baited smile again throw out,
Until the *right one* comes about!
Conquest is for the fair, like you,
Kind-hearted creatures, good and true.
Enslaved I am, or else my heart,
Resistless to thy shrine would start!

To Susie

THROUGH the depths of thy tender eyes,
   I read thy girlish heart;
And through thy silent, broken sighs,
   Its words to me impart.

O, silent spell! how sweet the charm,
   When the words are out of place!—
When thy dear head is on my arm,
   And I thy features trace!

O then, I seem to soar above,
   In some immortal sphere;
Where dwell eternal joy and love,
   And life's cares disappear!

Then let me here forever stay—
   Forever by thy side;
Where life is one eternal day,
   And thou, my joy and pride!

Adieu!

My task is done; go, gentle book,
    With all my hopes and fears:
Go win a sigh, a smile, a look—
    Perhaps a heart and tears!

Take rosy hope, and love, and joy,
    Upon thy fairy wing;
The lovers' leisure hours employ,
    And to their passions sing!

Thou hast a word for young and old—
    The beautiful and good;
The sunny beams within thy fold,
    Will be Love's dainty food!

Notes on the Poems

"To President Lincoln"

Abraham Lincoln published his executive order known as the Emancipation Proclamation on September 23, 1862. It declared that, effective January 1, 1863, the President would free all slaves in rebel-held portions of the Confederate States of America unless the secessionist states returned to their allegiance to the United States by that date. See, for example, Stephen B. Oates, *With Malice Toward None: The Life of Abraham Lincoln* (New York: Harper & Row, 1977), 319.

"Grant's First Election"

Ulysses S. Grant, hero to African Americans as the North's victorious Civil War military commander, first achieved election as President of the United States on November 3, 1868. He took office March 4, 1869. Interestingly, Florida's Republican-dominated legislature cancelled the popular election for the presidency in 1868, choosing instead to appoint the state's three electoral college members by law. See, for example, William S. McFeely, *Grant: A Biography* (New York: W. W. Norton, 1981), 283-84, 286; *Laws of Florida* (1868), 166-67; Canter Brown, Jr., *Florida's Black Public Officials, 1867-1924* (Tuscaloosa: University of Alabama Press, 1998), 17-18

"Stanzas on Cuba"

Although Cuba remained a possession of the Spanish Empire until the Spanish-American War of 1898, many of its residents long had struggled for their freedom. With Florida lying in such close proximity to the island, the state's residents watched developments there with interest. More than a few Floridians offered support that ranged from poetical expression such as that evidenced in these verses to money, supplies, and a willingness to fight. Particularly with respect to Menard's interest, in 1868 the *Junta Revolucionaria de la Isla de Cuba* launched what history has recorded as the Ten Years' War, basing its revolt partly upon opposition to Spanish protection of slavery. The bloody conflict ended in early 1878 when Spain promised to consider a range of reforms including slave emancipation. See, for example, Gonzalo de Quesada, *The War in Cuba* (Washington, D.C.: Liberty Publishing Co., 1896); Gerald E. Poyo, *"With All, and for the Good of All": The Emergence of Popular Nationalism in the Cuban Communities of the United States, 1848-1898* (Durham, N.C.: Duke University Press, 1989), 18-51; Ramon Eduardo Ruiz, *Cuba: The Making of A Revolution* (Amherst: University Of Massachusetts Press, 1968), 20.

"Waiting at Live Oak"

Through the 1870s, northeast and peninsular Florida's single rail link with Savannah and the North ran from Dupont, Georgia, to the Suwannee County seat of Live Oak. As a result, travelers such as John Willis Menard often found themselves forced to spend considerable time during lengthy layovers at the otherwise isolated town's train station. See George W. Pettengill, Jr., *The Story of the Florida Railroads, 1834-1903* (Boston: Railway & Locomotive Historical Society, Inc., and Baker Library, Harvard Business School, 1952), 28-30, 64; Larry Eugene Rivers and Canter Brown, Jr., *Laborers in the Vineyard of the Lord: The Beginnings of the AME Church in Florida, 1865-1895* (Gainesville: University Press of Florida, 2001), 64-65.

"To Madame Selika"

Madame Marie Selika Williams (c.1849-1937) was an acclaimed African American coloratura soprano, who toured Europe thrilling opera lovers and performing for royalty. She refused engagements in the segregated South, but was the first black artist to sing in the White House, where she gave a Green Room performance for President Hayes. She also gave a command performance in London for Queen Victoria. See Peter G. Davis, *The American Opera Singer: The Lives and Adventures of America's Great Singers in Opera from 1825 to the Present* (New York: Doubleday, 1997).

"On the Banks of the St. Johns"

The St. Johns River is the longest in Florida and one of the few American rivers to flow north. It originates in the marshes southwest of Cape Canaveral, running northward and eventually broadening to two miles in width as it turns eastward at Jacksonville, where it empties into the Atlantic Ocean.

"Charles Sumner"

The March 11, 1874, death of abolitionist leader and United States Senator Charles Sumner of Massachusetts profoundly saddened many of the nation's African Americans. The distinguished African Methodist Episcopal bishop Daniel A. Payne declared of him: "Never was a statesman truer and more faithful to his country. Never was a reformer more devoted to his principles. Never was a champion of human rights more loyal to the cause for which he labored, lived, and died." See, for example, Stephen Ward Angell, *Bishop Henry McNeal Turner and African-American Religion in the South* (Knoxville: University of Tennessee Press, 1992), 110, 118; Charles Spencer Smith, *A History of the African Methodist Episcopal Church* (Philadelphia: Book Concern of the A. M. E. Church, 1922), 123. On Sumner's life and career, see David Herbert Donald, *Charles Sumner* (New York: Da Capo Press, 1996).

"To General Grant"

General Ulysses S. Grant was sent by Lincoln's successor, President Andrew Johnson, on a fact-finding tour of the South in 1865. There Grant observed for himself the resurgence of discrimination and the renewal of violence. Known as a "peace-loving general," he found the situation profoundly disturbing, placing him increasingly in alliance with "radical" Republicanism and making him an obvious candidate for the 1868 presidential election. Grant supported full enfranchisement for blacks and sought to enforce the fourteenth and fifteeth amendments. These concerns also led to his support for the passage of the Force Acts of 1870-71. Again, see McFeely, *Grant*.

"In Mama's Bed"

Menard's youngest daughter Mary (sometimes spelled "Marie") answered to the nicknames "Mamie" and "Pet."

"Free Cuba"

See note on "Stanzas on Cuba," page 83.

"Frederick Douglass"

Frederick Douglass, born a Maryland slave in 1817-1818, emerged as the nation's premier African American abolitionist writer, journalist, and speaker of the antebellum era. He died at his fifteen-acre estate in Washington, D.C., on February 20, 1895. On Douglass's life, see Benjamin Quarles, *Frederick Douglass* (Washington, D.C.: Associated Publishers, 1948); Philip S. Foner, *The Life and Writings of Frederick Douglass*, 4 vols. (New York: International Publishers, 1950-1955); Frederick Douglass, *Narrative of the Life of Frederick Douglass an American Slave Written By Himself*, ed. by David W. Blight (Boston: Bradford Press of St. Martin's Press, 1993).

"In Memorium"

Until Governor Ossian Bingley Hart's death in March 1874, Florida's Republican party had maintained his ascendency over state affairs. Factional infighting thereafter drained party strength to the point that on February 11, 1875, some Republicans joined with Democrats to elect Democrat Charles W. Jones to the United States Senate over Republican Horatio S. Bisbee. As late as the legislature's twenty-second poll held on February 10, Bisbee stood within five votes of victory. See, for example, Jerrell H. Shofner, *Nor Is It Over Yet, Florida in the Era of Reconstruction, 1863-1877* (Gainesville: University of Florida Press, 1974), 296; Canter Brown, Jr., *Ossian Bingley Hart, Florida's Loyalist Reconstruction Governor* (Baton Rouge: Louisiana State University Press, 1997), 294-300; Tallahassee *Weekly Floridian*, February 16, 1875; *Florida House Journal* (1875), 227-29.

"On the Death of Wm. Lloyd Garrison"

Abolitionist editor William Lloyd Garrison, who was born on December 10, 1805, died on May 24, 1879. See John L. Thomas, *The Liberator: William Lloyd Garrison* (Boston: Little, Brown, 1963).

"The Solid South"

Following Democratic victories in Florida, South Carolina, and Louisiana state elections in late 1876, Democrats found themselves in control of state governments throughout the former Confederacy. According to historian Rayford W. Logan, the term "Solid South" quickly came into common usage to describe the party's grasp on regional political power. Rayford W. Logan, *The Negro in the United States* (Princeton, N.J.: D. Van Nostrand Co., 1957), 43.

"Good-bye! Off for Kansas"

The ebbing of Republican political power in the South during the mid-1870s convinced thousands of African Americans to seek their fortunes outside the region. This "exodus," as the movement came to be called, claimed Kansas as a favorite destination. Those who made the journey carried the name "exodusters." The cause remained a potent one in Florida at the time John Willis Menard's *Lays in Summer Lands* made its way into print, as illustrated by a mass meeting held on the subject at Tallahassee in October 1879. Sponsors of the gathering included many black political leaders well known to Menard, including John Wallace, John N. Stokes, and William F. Thompson. Wallace later penned the first history of Florida's Reconstruction-era experience. See Nell Irvin Painter, *Exodusters: Black Migration to Kansas After Reconstruction* (New York: Knopf, 1977); Tallahassee *Weekly Floridian*, October 28, 1879; John Wallace, *Carpetbag Rule in Florida* (Jacksonville: Da Costa Printing and Publishing House, 1888).

"Lines Written in 'Pet's' Album"

As noted, Menard's youngest daughter Mary (Marie) received the nickname "Pet." She married James B. Kinloch in Jacksonville in 1889.

"Phillis Wheatley"

African American poet Phillis Wheatley, who lived from about 1753 to 1884, was born in Senegal, but had arrived in Boston, Massachusetts, by the early 1760s. Manumitted from slavery in 1773, she traveled to London, England, to recuperate from illness. There, her first volume of verse *Poems on Various Subjects, Religious and Moral* was published. She returned to the American colonies the following year, but survived only for one decade. See, for example, W. Augustus Low and Virgil A. Clifts, comps., *Encyclopedia of Black America* (New York: Da Capo Press, n.d.), 852; Langston Hughes and Arna Bontemps, eds., *The Poetry of the Negro: 1746-1949* (New York: Doubleday and Company, 1949), 4, 6-11.

⊰ Essays ⊱

LAYS IN SUMMER LANDS.

POEMS,

BY J. WILLIS MENARD.

WITH THE

PRESS NOTICES OF HIS SPEECH AND HIS
APPEARANCE IN CONGRESS.

WASHINGTON:
ENTERPRISE PUBLISHING COMPANY.
1879.

The first edition's title page.

John Willis Menard and
Lays in Summer Lands

In the years that followed the Civil War's end, one of Florida's and the South's outstanding African American leaders authored a fascinating series of evocative poems that, in 1879, he compiled for publication. Remarkable for their apparent simplicity, John Willis Menard's verses nonetheless well reflected the issues and themes of his life and times as he understood them. An active politician and newspaper editor, poet Menard touched upon economic, political, and social conditions, as well as upon sentiments of the heart. In doing so, he desired—as did numerous other black authors of the time—to open public eyes in recognition of the skills and talents possessed by African Americans, especially including the ability to express themselves by producing written works of outstanding quality, originality, and imagination. Menard accomplished even more. Through publication of *Lays in Summer Lands*, he articulated the complexities, challenges, and exaltations of African American life in Florida during the Reconstruction and post-Reconstruction eras in a voice that continues to resonate into the twenty-first century.[1]

Although emerging forces of racial prejudice, political oppression, and Jim Crow discrimination soon effectively lowered a veil of obscurity over Menard's writings, for a brief time following the publication of *Lays in Summer Lands* his poetry achieved broad acclaim in Florida. Even his political enemies acknowledged as much. The leading partisan organ of the state's white conservatives, the Tallahassee *Semi-Weekly Floridian*, conceded its quality. From the state's largest city, the white editor of the Key West *Key of the Gulf* expressed a similar opinion. "We have examined the work and have no hesitation in pronouncing it an excellent one," he declared. "Some of the sentiments contained therein are of a superior order."[2]

At the outset, it should be noted that Menard's poetry continued a long and honorable tradition. By 1879, creative black authors in the United States had been expressing themselves and describing their world through artistic and romantic writings for more than one century. The respected historian John Hope Franklin has characterized the efforts of many of them as a "search for intellectual and spiritual independence." The poetic legacy, in particular, can be traced as far back as the mid-eighteenth century

Phillis Wheatley.

with the writings of Phillis Wheatley and Jupiter Hammon. Exposed to evangelical Protestantism as opposed to secular learning and heavily influenced by the Great Awakening, Wheatley and Hammon dealt largely, as might be expected, with religious questions and subjects. Hammon—held in slavery on Long Island, New York—offered "An Evening Thought. Salvation by Christ, with Penitential Cries" in 1761. Seventeen years later he added one of numerous other works, "To Miss Phillis Wheatley." By then, Wheatley's renown had spread far and wide. Her first published poem, "On the Death of the Reverend George Whitefield," had been published in 1770. Her book *Poems on Various Subjects, Religious and Moral* had followed within only a few years.[3]

Other black poets of the early and mid-nineteenth century built on the foundations laid by Hammon and Wheatley. North Carolina slave George Moses Horton, for instance, published widely and gained a substantial audience. To name one of his works, Horton's volume *The Hope of Liberty* was issued in 1829. Still, he numbered just one among many African Americans whose poems proved worthy of publication during the era. Among the others, Bishop Daniel A. Payne of the African Methodist Episco-

Frances E. W. Harper.　　　　　Daniel A. Payne.

pal Church, in 1850 ushered his book *Pleasures and Other Miscella-neous Poems* into print. Importantly for this discussion, Payne su-pervised the organization of his church in Florida in the years im-mediately following emancipation and served eventually as the state's bishop. As an elderly man the venerable churchman spent his winters at Jacksonville, where he and John Willis Menard came to know each other well. Similarly, Frances Ellen Watkins Harper crafted verse that drew on her recollections of life and race. *Poems on Miscellaneous Subjects*, perhaps her most-famous such effort, ap-peared in 1854. In the post-Civil War era Harper on several occa-sions campaigned in Florida on behalf of civil rights for African Americans, women's rights, and temperance, usually in coopera-tion with the AME Church. Although no documentary evidence establishes the fact conclusively, Harper likely encountered Menard during at least one of her visits to the state.[4]

Yet another early poet who associated closely with the AME Church influenced Menard in a meaningful manner. Thomas M. D. Ward began a four-year term as bishop of Florida in 1872, about the time that Menard arrived in the state. A dynamic leader, Ward returned for a second tour of duty in 1892. As an AME layman and as a political activist, Menard would have spent con-siderable time with the bishop, doubtlessly sharing their mutual love of poetry.[5] If not earlier, perhaps during those heady days of Reconstruction Menard first read and drew inspiration from Ward's "The Heroic Christian Warrior," written in the 1850s:

> My soul, the conflict grows severe,
> The troops of hell are drawing near—
> But the strong guard that for the fight
> Will guide thee to the worlds of light.
>
> Gird on thy arms, march to the field,
> With glittering blade and burnish'd shield;
> High floats the spotless flag of truth,
> Upborne by hands that never droop.
>
> The battle trump sounds long and loud,
> Bidding each warrior grasp his sword;
> Jehovah's great Eternal Son
> Will lead the fearless army on.
>
> Methinks I hear the glorious shout—
> The victory's won, the battle's fought,
> Emmanuel's troops have won the day—
> His foes have fled in wild dismay.
>
> No more the clarion sound we hear
> Thrilling each heart with hope and fear;
> The warrior wears the victor's palm
> High in the bright and better land.
>
> There in the realms of endless day
> Where stirring zephyrs lofty play,
> We'll stand amid the spotless throng
> And chant redemption's gladsome song.
>
> Cease not the strife, my blood-bought soul;
> Press onward to the blissful goal—
> Broad streams of everlasting light
> Will burst upon thy ravish'd sight.[6]

Complementing the efforts of churchmen such as Payne and Ward, the AME Church's organ *The Christian Recorder*—first issued on July 1, 1852–itself sponsored and encouraged African Americans, particularly African Methodists such as John Willis Menard, to express their souls and minds in verse. The paper's first number carried Bishop Payne's "Dedicatory Lines to the Recorder," plus a second poem. F. E. W. Harper's "The Soul" and "The Dying Christian" debuted there in 1853, as did Thomas M. D. Ward's "Lines

Thomas M. D. Ward.

on the Death of Rev. E. C. Africanus" and "The Heroic Christian Warrior." Over the decades countless other black-authored poems on a wide variety of subjects and expressing a broad range of sentiments reached their audience through the *Recorder*'s columns. During Menard's Florida residence and up to publication of *Lays in Summer Lands*, the weekly could boast the distinction of being the largest circulation African American newspaper in the state.[7]

Thus, from the earliest days of freedom in Florida, many African Americans benefitted from access to–and enjoyed the reading of–poetry and other literature written for them by other African Americans. This trend increased as black journalists and black newspapers proliferated. Probably the state's first black journalist and major author, John T. Shuften, arrived in Florida from Augusta, Georgia, where he had established the *Colored American* in 1866. By the early 1870s he had gained employment at Jacksonville's white-owned *Florida Union*. Shuften stepped into a wider celebrity in 1877 when a Jacksonville publisher issued his *A Colored Man's Exposition of the Acts and Doings of the Radical Party South, From 1865 to 1876, and Its Probable Overthrow by Presi-*

John Wallace.

dent *Hayes' Southern Policy.* Over the years Shuften gravitated southward with the trend of immigration down the peninsula to the growing community of Orlando. By 1893 he served as principal of its academy for African American children while continuing to thunder in print at the Republican party's betrayal of black Americans.[8]

Shuften pioneered the writing of book-length commentary by African American Floridians on politics and government, but others quickly trod the path he had set with substantive results. John Wallace deserves particular notice in that regard. A Union army veteran from North Carolina, Wallace held office during the late 1860s and 1870s as a state representative, state senator, and justice of the peace. In fact, during its 1874 session he shared membership in the Florida house of representatives with John Willis Menard. Disillusioned by what he perceived as the corruption of the Reconstruction process, though, Wallace in the 1880s penned *Carpetbag Rule in Florida: The Inside Workings of the Reconstruction of Civil Government in Florida After the Close of the Civil War.* Wallace intended several objects by publishing the book. Among them, he noted, "This work is further intended to prove that notwithstanding the blunders of the ex-slaveholder towards the colored people, the deception and betrayal by the carpet baggers of the colored people into the hands of their former masters, yet they, like the thunder-driven oak, have defied the storm which has now spent its terrific force, and like a caravan of determined pioneers cutting out highways in a new country, the Negro is laying the foundation for a civilization that shall be fully equal in every respect to that of any other race or people." As it turned out, *Carpetbag Rule in Florida* set the tone for works on

Florida's Reconstruction past for several generations.[9]

As should not seem too surprising by now, John Wallace also prided himself as a poet, often reading his works on public occasions. At Tallahassee's seventeenth anniversary celebration of the Emancipation Proclamation, he offered the following verse written especially for the day's festivities:

> Freedom, thou welcome spirit of Love,
> Whence and from where didst thou begin?
> Thou from God's bosom as a dove
> Didst seek the earth to vanquish sin.
> Before the land and skies were made
> Thy spirit hovered o'er the deep,
> And when God earth's foundation laid,
> Did enter man when yet asleep.
> As he arose from dust to flesh,
> Near him wast thou where e'er he went;
> Though cast from Eden's garden fresh,
> Thou wast with him in sorrow bent.
> And still wast thou all through
> Despotic ages past and gone,
> And as a brother e'er proved true—
> Thy light 'mid darkness ever shone.
> When Pharaoh Israel's children held
> Four hundred years abject, enslaved,
> To free them Egypt was impelled,
> Though then was gained the land they craved.
>
> America thought thee to evade,
> And to the South her slaves she sold;
> But through power she was made
> To yield to thee this great stronghold.
> Though here was called unto thy aid
> Grim war, the court of last appeal—
> And North and South each other braved,
> Yet now they both thy blessings feel.
> There were four million souls and more
> Of Africans in slavery bound,
> They sought they crown 'mid trials sore,
> Two hundred years, and then 'twas found.

Mankind has ne'er contented been
Where slavery's cruel sway was held.
'Twas giant Freedom fought the sin
Till all its darkness was dispelled.
Go sound the trumpet, ring the bell!
Just seventeen years ago to-day
Sweet Freedom wrested us from hell
And put an end to slavery's sway.[10]

Black journalists at white-owned newspapers aided expression of African American sentiments through creative writing, but so, too, did black-owned Florida newspapers. Congressman Josiah Walls purchased the first such paper—the *New Era*—at Gainesville in 1873. Interestingly, Walls and Menard often found themselves on different sides of the Republican party divide, and speculation remains irresistible as to whether his adversary's control of a newspaper prompted Menard to think in terms of editing his own journal.[11]

In any event, over time Florida's numerous black-owned newspapers followed the lead of the *Christian Recorder*, and not coinci-

Josiah Walls.

dentally of many white-owned organs of the period, by featuring the work of local poets. While only a handful of issues of Florida's black newspapers of the late 1800s remain extant, they contain examples of the sometimes skillful and moving submissions. One such work, concerned with society's treatment of blacks, appeared in the Pensacola *Florida Sentinel* in 1900. Here,

Cornelius Wilmot Taylor expressed herself about race, ignorance, gloom, and prejudice in American society:

"A Voice Out of the Past"

Oh the night has been long and the way has been hard
For the men who have toiled for their kind;
The rack and the dungeon have been their reward,
And, [bequeathed?] an ignominious mind.
The Christ has been crucified, martyrs been burned,
The philosophers tortured and slain;
But their spirits once more to the earth have returned,
And their truths have arisen again.

By the lives of these heroes be guided today,
As brothers and on with the fight,
Be strong, be patient, not faint by the way,
Till the world is brought 'round to the right.
From the ignorance, prejudice, darkness and gloom,
The injustice and wrong of the past,
We have risen till now we can see the bloom
In the morn on the hill tops at last.

The way by the blood of the prophets was wet,
But they toiled not and died not in vain;
And the words of these prophets are guiding us yet
To the triumphs we shall yet attain.
The night of the ages gives away to the dawn
While the race is yet in its youth;
So face the future, my brothers and on
Till the world is brought over to truth.[12]

The literary and cultural sensibility that matured in Florida within the arena of such forms of expression reached its Reconstruction and early post-Reconstruction era peak with the publication of *Lays in Summer Lands*, but Menard's achievement involved more than the triumph of his verse. His example encouraged and inspired creativity on a far-greater scale, with numerous other talented black Floridians publishing poems that soon commanded national and international attention. Timothy Thomas Fortune, to cite a first example, entered life as a slave in Jackson

T. Thomas Fortune   Emanuel Fortune.

County, Florida. His father Emanuel Fortune served in the state legislature before relocating in the early 1870s to Jacksonville, where the family lived when Menard arrived in the state. The younger Fortune attained his schooling within an environment in which Menard played a key role, although, as will be seen, they came to disagree on a number of key issues. Tim Fortune went on to gain fame and influence as the driving force behind newspapers such as the *New York Freeman* and the *New York Age*. He earned a reputation as a poet, as well. Of special note, in 1905 he offered *Dreams of Life*, a volume that contained a series of poems reflecting his life experiences in Florida and in the nation as a whole.[13]

A generation later Eatonville native Zora Neale Hurston also wrote moving poetry about Florida, its locales, and its people. Often referred to as an exemplar of the Harlem Renaissance, Hurston, in one imminent historian's words, proved "both brilliant and prolific." Her writing vividly reflected Sunshine State roots, evoking, as had Menard two generations earlier, a particular sense of place as well as of person. Hurston's autobiographical *Dust Tracks on a Road*, issued in 1942, could not help but lapse into poetry as memories of past experiences flooded back to her over the years. Polk County, located in the peninsula's heart, served as one of her special centers of inspiration. Of the place, she expressed in her intensely human and forceful style:

Yea! Polk County!
You don't know Polk County like I do
Anybody been there, tell you same thing, too.
Eh, rider, rider!
Polk County, where the water like cherry wine.[14]

Zora Neale Hurston.

Perhaps the most revered legacy of John Willis Menard's poetical influence came with the works of James Weldon Johnson. "I have a very clear recollection of J. [W.] Menard," Johnson declared in his autobiography *Along This Way*. The Jacksonville native son became, as did Zora Neale Hurston, a central figure in shaping the Harlem Renaissance with works such as *God's Trombones* and the provocative novel *The Autobiography of an Ex-Coloured Man*. His classic compilation *The Book of American Poetry* debuted in 1922. Many of Johnson's poems— "O Black and Unknown Bards," "Fifty Years," "The Creation," "Since You Went Away," and "My City," for example—were read and recited by many others during the 1920s and afterwards. Doubtlessly, though, his "Lift Every Voice and Sing" became the most significant piece of poetry Johnson would author. Later known as the Negro National Anthem, he wrote it in 1900 to celebrate Abraham Lincoln's birthday. Its words, which reveal so much about the

James Weldon Johnson.

trials and tribulations blacks faced in America during the early twentieth century, offer a truly worthy legacy of *Lays in Summer Lands*:

> Lift every voice and sing
> Till earth and heaven ring,
> Ring with the harmonies of Liberty;
> Let our rejoicing rise
> High as the listening skies,
> Let it resound loud as the rolling sea.
> Sing a song full of the faith that the dark past has taught us,
> Sing a song full of the hope that the present has brought us,
> Facing the rising sun of our new day begun
> Let us march on till victory is won.
>
> Stony the road we trod,
> Bitter the chastening rod,
> Felt in the days when hope unborn had died;
> Yet with a steady beat,
> Have not our weary feet
> Come to the place for which our father sighed?
> We have come over a way that with tears has been watered,
> We have come, treading our path through the blood of the slaughtered,
> Out from the gloomy past,
> Till now we stand at last,
> Where the white gleam of our bright star is cast,
>
> God of our weary years,
> God of our silent tears,
> Thou who has brought us thus far on the way,
> Thou who has by Thy might,
> Led us into the light,
> Keep us forever in the path, we pray.
> Lest our feet stray from the places, our God, where we met Thee,
> Lest, our hearts drunk with the wine of the world, we forget Thee;

Shadowed beneath Thy hand,
May we forever stand
True to our God,
True to our native land.[15]

To appreciate *Lays In Summer Lands* fully, the reader naturally benefits from an understanding of J. Willis Menard. Who was he? And, how did his poetry reflect his life experiences? What, if anything, do the poems suggest about the meaning of that life, as well as about his political, social, and economic attitudes during the post-Civil War period?

As will be discussed further in the succeeding essay, Menard's saga began far from Florida. Born in Kaskaskia, Illinois, on April 3, 1838, of "colored Creole French" parentage, he may have been the only son born to this union. One northern newspaper later described him as "a man of good stature and stout body, young and pleasant-looking in the face, the features of which, though heavy, are mobile and vivacious, while the color is a dark brown." Other sources simply described him as a calm, self-composed, educated mulatto. James Weldon Johnson thought him far more imposing. Menard, Johnson recalled, "look[ed] a good deal like the pictures of Alexandre Dumas."[16]

With few records of his origins and early life coming to light, Menard's background remain shrouded in obscurity. Several things, though, seem certain. First, several sources indicate that Menard remained on a Kaskaskia farm until the age of eighteen when he attended an abolitionist school in Sparta, Illinois. Second, he had not been a slave. And third, in 1858 at the age of twenty-one, Menard traveled to Ohio to matriculate at Iberia College. Due to limited funds, he found himself forced to drop out after pursuing studies for only two or three terms. However short, Menard's college stint put him in good stead for a career as a black political leader and writer.[17]

The future poet evidenced those leanings early on. He took up race advocacy on the public stage prior to the Civil War's beginning. This led to publication of his first work *An Address to the Free Colored People of Illinois* in 1860. At the time he maintained a residence in Randolph County. Two years into the conflict, the activist obtained a clerkship in the Interior department in Washington, D.C. He thus became, in 1862, the first black to hold such a position. Because Menard favored the immigration and subsequent colonization of blacks to foreign lands, the government sent him to investigate the Central American country of Belize as a possible solution to the "Negro problem." Nothing resulted from his investigation, although the journey led Menard to marriage with his Jamaican wife Elizabeth. Still, the young man became well known in Washington's official circles.[18]

Menard in 1865 traveled to New Orleans, the birth place of his parents, with landmark consequences. He intended initially to participate in the reconstruction of Louisiana's government. Soon after his arrival in the Crescent City, an eager Menard took office as an inspector of customs and later served as commissioner of streets. Eventually he edited the New Orleans *Free South*, which became the New Orleans *Standard*. In 1867 he published a pamphlet, *Black and white. No party-no creed*. The next year, using the family name to his advantage, Menard campaigned for and secured the Republican nomination for the unexpired term of deceased Congressman James Mann. On election day he received the clear majority of votes cast, a fact that should have made him the first African American to serve in the United States Congress. Contesting the election and Menard's claim to the vacant seat, his opponent Caleb S. Hunt successfully appealed to the Committee on Elections of the United States House of Representatives. Congressman James A. Garfield—later president of the United States—insisted "That it was too early to admit a Negro to the U.S. Congress, and that the seat be declared vacant, and the salary ($5,000) be divided equally between the two contestants." A majority of the committee agreed with Garfield. They declared the case closed and thereby robbed Menard of a Congressional seat that he clearly had won.[19]

Menard did achieve a signal distinction in his quest to be seated in the United States House of Representatives. He became, in 1869, the first black to address the Congress. Because of

John Willis Menard speaking to Congress, February 27, 1869.

Menard's respect for the office for which he had been elected and the desire to represent the Louisianians who voted for him, he insisted on the opportunity. Much as would be true of his poems, Menard's eloquence and thoughtfulness shone through his words. Appealing to the senses and intellect of fellow congressmen, Menard asked that his race not be taken into account. He desired only, he declared, that the case be decided on its own merits, pointing out that Hunt had not received a majority of the votes nor had he complied with congressional requirements in serving him notice that the Louisiana seat would be contested.[20]

The ultimately unsuccessful initiative earned the claimant widespread praise. "Mr. Menard delivered what he had to say with a cool readiness and clearness that surprised everybody," the New York *Herald* reported, for example. The Washington (D.C.) *Daily Chronicle* agreed. "For the first time in history of Congress a colored man, on Saturday last, made a speech upon the floor of the House of Representatives, and that, too, in advocacy of his claim to a seat as a Representative of a portion of the American people," the paper informed its readers. "It is doubtful whether any one in the House could have commanded more attention from gentlemen on both sides of the House, and Mr. Menard acquitted himself so well as to elicit the congratulations of some of the most prominent Republicans in Congress, and his speech and bearing no doubt did much toward securing him fifty-seven votes for his admission to a seat."[21]

In the aftermath of the congressional rebuke, Menard left New Orleans somewhat frustrated and relocated to what he must have hoped would be the more congenial clime of Florida. He settled in 1871 at Jacksonville in Duval County. He had attained at the time the age of only thirty-three. With his talent as a former editor of two New Orleans newspapers, his education, and his political experience, he soon became a well-known politician and race leader in his newly adopted home. At least on the state level, Menard would find some success in politics where he failed without fault of his own in Louisiana.[22]

The ambitious politician and editor brought his wife Elizabeth and children with him to Jacksonville, and they helped to clear his path to future success. The young ones included Willis, Jr., Mary Jeannette, and Alice. Through them, Menard cemented his standing in the highest ranks of Florida's African American political and social circles. Alice, for instance, married Thomas Van Renssalaer Gibbs, a prominent Duval County politician and educator who was the son of the late Honorable Jonathan C. Gibbs, Secretary of State and Superintendent of Public Instruction. Mary would wed James S. Kinloch, whose prominent businessman father served on the Duval County school board.[23]

Jacksonville, Florida, in the 1870s.

Menard's participation in Florida politics began shortly after his arrival in Duval County, at a time when the African American role in state and local government was soaring thanks in good part to the coordinated efforts of AME clergymen and laymen. Florida had just sent its first black man, Josiah Walls, to the United States Congress, and optimism ran high. As one adherent put it at the time, "African Methodism is about to rule

John Robert Scott.

Florida." Menard first secured a political appointment in the Jacksonville post office, identifying clearly with the Republican Party in the state. He also associated as an editor with the Jacksonville *Florida Sun*. During the fall of 1873, he sought to fill a Duval County legislative vacancy created by the resignation of AME presiding elder John Robert Scott who had accepted appointment as United States collector of revenues. The following January Menard took his seat in the state legislature. Given that he had been in Florida only three years, Menard had accomplished much with little opposition.[24]

Menard's ambitions for higher office, on the other hand, met with furious opposition. The young man cast his eye in 1874 on a run for national office much as he had done in Louisiana. He focused on the second district congressional seat held by Josiah Walls. John R. Scott opted to make the race, as well. The resulting contest proved a very nasty affair. Walls and Scott both took Menard's challenge seriously and targeted him for heavy criticism. These men already knew a good deal about Menard's successful New Orleans race and his unsuccessful attempt to be seated in the Congress.[25]

Cries of impropriety and moral malfeasance quickly dominated the 1874 congressional campaign. Scott sought to push Menard out of the political race by revealing what he thought to be a scandal concerning Menard's involvement with a woman in New Orleans. Scott appeared to enjoy support from the Jacksonville *New South* and the Pensacola *Republican*, among other newspapers. Those organs also blasted Menard's character and wayward behavior in Louisiana. Were these allegations true? Menard, on his part, dismissed them as baseless. In a communication to the Jacksonville *Florida Union*, he declared:

> The statement in question is to the effect that I had "to skedaddle from Louisiana to avoid the vengeance of the law." Every person of common sense knows or ought to know that if a man commits a crime in any State and flees to another, he can immediately be apprehended, arrested, and taken back for trial by a requisition from the Governor of the State in which the crime is alleged to have been committed. The statement taken from the Picayune makes no direct charges against me, but simply says "it is alleged he was charged with outraging a woman of his own race."
>
> Were it not for the easy credulity of the public, more especially of my political enemies, I would take no notice of this matter. In justice to myself and friends I will state that about a year before I left New Orleans, a woman did prefer a charge against me, with the view, as it was very apparent from her conduct, of blackmailing. I appeared in answer to the charge, but the woman did not appear. The Attorney for the State, on the following day, entered a nol pros in the case, and the matter ended. I have sent to New Orleans for a transcript of the case for the benefit of my political enemies. This is the only charge ever preferred against me in my life, and my political enemies are welcome to all they can make of it. I have been in Florida for three years, and I leave it to those who know me to judge whether or not my conduct has been "outrageous."

Menard ended his letter by insisting that he had "as much right to hold office as anybody else." He continued, "Those who say I was compelled to leave Louisiana, are simply liars." What impact did the allegation have on Menard's campaign? No one will ever know for certain, but he dropped out of the race shortly after the alleged scandal surfaced.[26]

Menard clearly showed signs of frustration with the Republican Party, particularly the white northerners known as carpetbaggers, after his second attempt to gain national office. Already he had begun to blame the party for the lack of progress made by black Floridians. Throwing a challenge into Congressman Walls's own backyard, he condemned carpetbaggers in the columns of the *Gainesville Times* for denying blacks their rightful political roles. The activist would struggle with his sentiments about the Republican party, developing a love/hate relationship with its leadership that lasted for much of the rest of his life. Especially, Menard would accuse the party of claiming to represent the interests of blacks when it, in fact, had aligned with Democrats on decisions that stymied the progress of African Americans in the state and nation.[27]

Yet, Menard would seek the Republican nomination for the second congressional district for the second time in 1876. With the death of popular Republican governor Ossian B. Hart in 1874 and the subsequent re-emergence of Democratic power, many believed that Menard and other black republicans stood little chance of winning state or national office. Their assumptions proved correct. Neither Menard nor any of the other black candidates won a Florida congressional seat in 1876. The Democratic party strove mightily to "redeem" Florida and the rest of the South from the clutches of blacks, scalawags, and carpetbaggers. Even though Florida's white Republican gubernatorial candidate eventually would lose his election by only the smallest of margins, Menard abandoned his quest for the Republican nomination.[28]

He did not, on the other hand, give up his candidacy for the second district congressional seat. Menard simply announced as an Independent, although he supported some Republican candidates and also attended the Republican National Convention that year as a Florida delegate. Still, he now bitterly criticized the

Republican party for the contemptuous way it handled black members and for using race tactics to keep them under its control. "If the intelligent and thinking colored men in the South have any aspiration and hopes in the future," he proclaimed, "they will resist this outrage and fraud, and fight for equal representation and common justice." On election day disappointment again greeted the candidate. Menard's losing effort received the support of a minority of blacks and of very few whites.[29]

Even though when the dust settled following the 1876 elections the Democrats claimed power throughout the South, Menard yearned to continue his leadership roll and to remain on a public payroll. Probably because Menard's criticisms of Republican regulars had aided his candidacy, Democratic governor George F. Drew used his executive power in 1877 to reappoint the one-time legislator as a Duval County justice of the peace, a position to which Republican governor Marcellus Stearns had appointed him three years earlier. One can only speculate as to other reasons why a Democratic governor would appoint him to such a choice position. For one thing, Menard had appealed to white Floridians by stating that blacks needed to accept conditions "just as they are" and not continue to complain about their circumstances in Florida. He also had suggested that blacks needed to work with whites for the overall progress of the state.[30]

On his part, Menard continued to see himself and his career as headed for a higher level than that of a simple justice of peace in a single Florida county. Still hoping to be of service to the Republican party, he petitioned in late 1877 for an overseas assignment as an accredited United States diplomat to a foreign country. With letters of recommendation from many of Florida's most prominent Democrat and Republican politicians, Menard particularly sought appointment as minister to a South American country. One white Democratic Florida newspaper endorsed his bid but with a twist. "J. W. Menard, of Jacksonville, is in Washington after a consulship in some South American port," the Tallahassee *Weekly Floridian* observed. "Better send him to Liberia," the item continued. "A Washington dispatch says all

KEY WEST

This print from the period shows part of the island of Key West.

the consulates worth more than $2000 have been filled." Menard failed to get the consulship position. Instead he received a sinecure as a watchman in the post office department. Desiring a more lucrative position commensurate with his skills and status, he opted to relocate to Key West as an inspector of customs. The decision initially required him to leave his wife in Jacksonville. He later purchased residential property in Florida's largest town, and his wife joined him on the island.[31]

While he awaited a final decision on his customs position, the poet in Menard truly emerged. Although he had written verse for years, he now compiled *Lays in Summer Lands* for publication. While the work suggests much about its author's private life and thoughts as well as his political and social activism, some of its contents seem to show him looking toward his new home. One such poem, to cite an example, focuses on freedom in Cuba. The Spanish colony lay as close as ninety miles from Key West. While championing the cause of freedom there, Menard—as also was true of other black leaders—nonetheless feared that the United States might force its social and racial practices, ultimately including Jim Crow racial discrimination, on the island's residents.[32]

Once at beautiful, cosmopolitan, and racially tolerant Key West, the customs inspector found the island's heady atmosphere leading him to involvements beyond his not-too-taxing official position. He maintained an active political life, supporting the cause of Independents while preserving ties with the Republican establishment. Of special significance, the politician, public servant, author, and race man returned to his role as editor. In 1882 he took control of the Key West *Florida News* (sometimes called the *Island City News*) and used it as a platform from which to comment on questions of the day in the state and nation. The principal historian of Florida's black press praised his tenure. "Menard was the most influential black editor speaking for and to blacks in the 1880s," Jerrell Shofner concluded, "and his vigorous editorials were aimed at the political, economic, moral, and educational improvement of his race." The AME Church's *Christian Recorder* lauded his takeover. "J. Willis Menard & Son are to be congratulated on the appearance of the Key West News," it commented. "Success to the enterprise of our old friends." When Menard switched from a weekly to a semi-weekly publication schedule in 1884, the praise continued. "The Key West *News* will hereafter be issued semi-weekly," the New York *Globe* advised. "We congratulate our contemporary upon this evidence of substantial popularity."[33]

The popularity came from the fact that Menard refused to shy away from taking hard public positions, however controversial they might have seemed. He did so in straightforward language that became his hallmark. In 1884, for instance, Menard questioned in strong terms the state's commitment to equal educational opportunities for all residents. He asserted in his typical manner:

> The question of increased facilities of popular education for our children is paramount to all others, because it is the prime lever in our elevation. We must contend for the same facilities and advantages of education which the whites enjoy and make this the main plank in our political policy. If we must have separate schools and separate cars, let them have the same conveniences and advantages as those provided for the whites. "The same accommodations for the same money," should be our watch word.[34]

When the presidential election of 1884 ended disastrously for Republicans, Menard faced the loss of his customs position and determined, as a result, to relocate with his newspaper to Jacksonville. Within one year he announced that he had expanded its scope considerably. The name, henceforth, he proclaimed in 1886 would be the *Southern Leader*. "As the name News does not properly represent the nature and character of this paper," he explained, "we have made up our minds to begin the new year with the more appropriate name of *The Southern Leader*, under which name we shall continue to battle for the rights and interest of our people." As the political situation deteriorated for Florida blacks, Menard clearly desired that his readers know that he and his newspaper would take the lead in the state in covering news that concerned them and advocating causes in their best interest.[35]

During the mid-1880s Menard continued to flirt with the Independent Movement but remained in the end largely loyal to the national Republican party. At the local level, he pushed for the election of Independents with the assistance of the Republican party. At the national level, he urged blacks to support Republican candidates who stood a chance of winning the presidency. His *Southern Leader* editorials alternated between supporting and damning the party. In one instance he used his newspaper to support Republican son-in-law Thomas V. Gibbs's bid for office in Duval County while condemning Republicans throughout the state for consorting with Democrats at the expense of blacks. Menard ensured, as well, that the *Southern Leader* chronicled the rising tide of racial violence, lynchings, and wholesale disenfranchisement of blacks in Florida and throughout the South. As a consequence, his subscription rolls carried a considerable number of subscriber names from outside Florida.[36]

During the *Southern Leader* years, Menard developed a friendly but continuing dispute with fellow poet and editor T. Thomas Fortune (as mentioned, a Florida native) of the New York *Freeman* and, by 1888, the New York *Age* on the tactics blacks should employ to fight racism, violence, and discrimination in America.

Despite the lynchings throughout the South during the 1880s and 1890s, Menard still believed that blacks were making progress in the region. He disagreed, therefore, with Fortune's proposed formation of the Afro-American National League to unite blacks to fight for their civil rights. Menard argued that Fortune's criticisms of the southern whites from his New York office did "no good, neither do they solve our problems" here in the South. As it turned out, Fortune's Afro-American National League never received the support of blacks and folded several years after its incipience. Interestingly, the pace of tragic events caught up with the debate. Menard eventually moved closer to Fortune's point of view, concurring that the Afro-American National League would serve as an effective forum to voice the concerns of blacks.[37]

Menard persisted in political involvements but not as a candidate or officeholder. In 1888 he initially supported Senator John Sherman for the Republican presidential nomination but switched to Benjamin Harrison's side once he received the nod. At this point, Menard seemed to offer support to any Republican candidate who could defeat his Democratic opponent. Harrison narrowly won the election, but his presidency did little to improve the status of blacks who still largely supported the Republican party. By 1889, Menard saw that blacks and whites were "drifting further apart from each other every year." He summed up his increasing disillusionment with his party by arguing that it would likely do less and less to protect the rights of blacks through enforcement of the Fourteenth and Fifteenth Amendments.[38]

Beyond Republican and Democratic party politics, temperance or prohibition had emerged as a hot political issue during the 1880s. For Menard, the movement posed questions that he seemingly desired to avoid. Given that much of the state remained a free-wheeling frontier region from the 1820s into the twentieth century, alcohol consumption represented a way of life for many black and white Floridians. Still, many black churches joined the temperance movement to rid the state of alcoholic beverages. With all the other critical issues facing blacks at the time, Menard perhaps did not want take on an issue regarding which he clearly would lose from the outset. As one newspaper put it:

> Editor Menard is afraid that a discussion of the merits of Prohibition will hurt the Republican party of Florida, and prohibits such discussion, because, as he says, "We are opposed to bringing Prohibition into politics."[39]

By late 1888 the days of Menard's editorial prominence grew short. During a yellow fever epidemic he suspended the operations of his newspaper and left Jacksonville. When he returned shortly thereafter, he could not revive his newspaper. Some Jacksonville residents, it must be considered, may have questioned his loyalty or commitment to the city after his hasty departure. Needing employment, Menard beseeched the Harrison administration for a consulship to any South American country. When he saw that his hopes were not to be realized, he accepted a clerkship in the census office in Washington, D.C.[40]

There, Menard remained active in the Republican party. He helped to establish the Southern States Colored Republican Association, an organization formed "to disseminate wholesome political information among colored voters and to solidify young colored men of the nation to advance Republican principles." He also tried to re-establish a monthly magazine, the *National American*. The publication proved short lived due to competition from numerous black publications already rooted in the city.

Menard died at Washington, D.C. on October 8, 1893, at the age of fifty-five.[41]

Word of Menard's passing soon passed to Florida's towns, cities, and countryside. The Jacksonville *Florida Times-Union* eulogized him as "a man of brains and education [who] . . . had some reputation as a newspaper man, poet and politician . . . a good friend and wise counsellor to his race." The Pensacola *Daily News* noted, "He was a writer and a scholar and exercised considerable influence among people of his race." His old arch-opponent the Tallahassee *Weekly Floridian* at least acknowledged him as "a prominent colored man."[42]

No matter how one may describe John Willis Menard's political and journalistic careers, his book *Lays In Summer Lands* remains to us today as his principal legacy. A treasure to behold, it offers a rare if not unique glimpse at its author and of the society in which he lived. Menard chose to end the work with a short verse that he entitled "Adieu!" It serves as a fitting epitaph:

My task is done; go, gentle book,
With all my hopes and fears:
Go win a smile, a sigh, a look—
Perhaps a heart and tears!

Take rosy hope, and love, and joy,
Upon thy fairy wing;
The lovers' leisure hours employ,
And to their passions sing!

Thou hast a word for young and old—
The beautiful and good;
The sunny beams within they fold,
Will be Love's dainty food!

A Florida forest near Jacksonville.

Notes

1 J. Willis Menard, *Lays in Summer Lands: Poems by J. Willis Menard* (Washington, D.C.: Enterprise Publishing Company, 1879).

2 New York *Globe*, June 2, 1883; Tallahassee *Semi-Weekly Floridian*, July 16, 1880.

3 John Hope Franklin and Alfred A. Moss, Jr., *From Slavery to Freedom, A History of African Americans: Seventh Edition* (New York: McGraw-Hill, Inc., 1994), 92-94. See also Darlene Clark Hine, William C. Hine, and Stanley Harrold, *The African-American Odyssey* (Upper Saddle River, N.J.: Prentice Hall, 2000), 61-62, 78-93, 106, 152-53, 216, 220, 371; Langston Hughes and Arna Bontemps, eds., *The Poetry of the Negro: 1746-1949* (New York: Doubleday and Company, 1949), 4, 6-11.

4 Franklin and Moss, *From Slavery to Freedom*, 163-64; Hughes and Bontemps, *Poetry of the Negro*, 6-11; Larry Eugene Rivers and Canter Brown, Jr., *Laborers in the Vineyard of the Lord: The Beginnings of the AME Church in Florida, 1865-1895* (Gainesville: University Press of Florida, 2001), 24-25, 32-34, 37-38, 45, 67, 73, 76, 125, 130, 142-160; Canter Brown, Jr., "Bishop Payne and Resistance to Jim Crow in Florida During the 1880s," *Northeast Florida History* 2 (1994): 23-40; George F. Bragg, *Men of Maryland* (Baltimore: Church Advocate Press, 1914), 64-78; Savannah *Daily Republican*, May 1, 1870.

5 Rivers and Brown, *Laborers in the Vineyard of the Lord*, 80, 84-87, 89-100, 108, 113, 185-94.

6 Bragg, *Men of Maryland*, 109-110.

7 Daniel A. Payne, *History of the African Methodist Episcopal Church* (Nashville: A. M. E. Sunday-School Union, 1891), 297-305.

8 Jerrell H. Shofner, "Florida," in *The Black Press in the South, 1865-1979*, ed. by Henry Lewis Suggs (Westport, Conn.: Greenwood Press, 1983), 91-92; Richard H. Abbot, "The Republican Party Press in Reconstruction Georgia, 1867-1874," *Journal of Southern History* 61 (November 1995): 727; John T. Shuften, *A Colored Man's Exposition of the Acts and Doings of the Radical Party South, From 1865 to 1876, and Its Probable Overthrow by President Hayes' Southern Policy* (Jacksonville: Gibson and Dennis Steam and Job Printers, 1877); Jacksonville *Florida Times-Union*, August 19, 1892; Jacksonville *Evening Telegram*, February 10, 1893.

9 John Wallace, *Carpetbag Rule in Florida: The Inside Workings of the Reconstruction of Civil Government in Florida After the Close of the Civil War* (Jacksonville: Da Costa Printing and Publishing House, 1888; reprint ed., Kennesaw, Ga.: Continental Book Company, 1959), 4; Canter Brown, Jr., *Florida's Black Public Officials, 1867-1924* (Tuscaloosa: University of Alabama

Press, 1998), 134-35. On the writing of *Carpetbag Rule in Florida*, see also James C. Clark, "John Wallace and the Writing of Reconstruction History," *Florida Historical Quarterly* 67 (April 1989): 409-427.

10 Wallace, *Carpetbag Rule in Florida*, 26-27.

11 Shofner, "Florida," 91-92; Peter D. Klingman, *Josiah Walls, Florida's Black Congressman of Reconstruction* (Gainesville: University of Florida Press, 1976), 53-54, 60.

12 Pensacola *Florida Sentinel*, January 26, 1900.

13 Hine, Hine, and Harrold, *African-American Odyssey*, 363, 380; Brown, *Florida's Black Public Officials*, 88-89. On Timothy Thomas Fortune, see Emma Lou Thornbrough, *T. Thomas Fortune, Militant Journalist* (Chicago: University of Chicago Press, 1972); Cyrus Field Adams, "Timothy Thomas Fortune: Journalist, Author, Lecturer, Agitator," *The Colored American Magazine* 4 (February 1902): 224-26.

14 Jane Anderson Jones and Maurice J. O'Sullivan, eds., *Florida In Poetry: A History of the Imagination* (Sarasota: Pineapple Press, 1995), xiii-xix; Franklin and Moss, *From Slavery to Freedom*, 361-80; Maxine D. Jones and Kevin M. McCarthy, *African Americans in Florida* (Sarasota: Pineapple Press, Inc., 1993), 78-79; Zora Neale Hurston, *Dust Tracks on a Road* (New York: Harper & Row, 1942); Freddie Wright, "Excerpts from 'Dust Tracks on a Road' Tell Early Black History," *Polk County Historical Quarterly* 9 (April 1983): 4-5; P. J. Brownlee, "Where de Water Drink Lak Cherry Wine: The Importance of Zora Neale Hurston's Work in Polk County, Florida," *Polk County Historical Quarterly* 27 (June 2000): 1-3, 7.

15 James Weldon Johnson, *Along This Way: The Autobiography of James Weldon Johnson* (New York: Penguin Books, 1990), 58, 154-55; Hughes and Bontemps, *The Poetry of the Negro*, 23-32; Franklin and Moss, *From Slavery to Freedom*, 365-67.

16 New Orleans *Daily Picayune*, March 28, 1874; Menard, *Lays in Summer Lands*, 6-14; Johnson, *Along This Way*, 58.

17 New York *Globe*, June 2, 1883; Thomas V. Gibbs, "John Willis Menard: The First Colored Congressman-Elect," *A. M. E. Church Review* 3 (April 1887), 426-32; Bess Beatty, "John Willis Menard: A Progressive Black in Post-Civil Florida," *Florida Historical Quarterly*, 59 (October 1980); 123-143. For a comprehensive account of slavery in Florida, see Larry Eugene Rivers, *Slavery In Florida: Territorial Days to Emancipation* (Gainesville: University Press of Florida, 2000).

18 John Willis Menard, *An Address to the Free Colored People of Illinois by J. W. Menard of Randolph County, Ill.* (N.p., 1860); New York *Globe*, June 2, 1883; Gibbs, "John Willis Menard," 426-32.

19 New York *Globe*, June 2, 1883; New Orleans *Daily Picayune*, March 28, 1874; Thomas V. Gibbs, "John Willis Menard," *A. M. E. Church Review*

3 (April 1887), 427; Edith Menard, "John Willis Menard, First Negro Elected to the U.S. Congress, First Negro to Speak in the U.S. Congress," *Negro History Bulletin* 18 (December 1964), 53; John Willis Menard, *Black and white. No party-no creed* (N.p., 1867?).

20 New York *Herald* and Worcester *Spy* as cited in New York *Globe*, June 2, 1883; Gibbs, "John Willis Menard," 426-32; Beatty, "John Willis Menard," 124; Joe Gray Taylor, *Louisiana Reconstructed, 1863-1877* (Baton Rouge: Louisiana State University Press, 1974), 172-73.

21 Gibbs, "John Willis Menard," 427-31.

22 New York *Globe*, June 2, 1883; Brown, *Florida's Black Public Officials, 1867-1924*, 20, 26, 30, 32, 36, 39, 56-57, 60, 62, 66, 69, 110; Jerrell H. Shofner, *Nor Is It Over Yet: Florida in the Era of Reconstruction, 1863-1877* (Gainesville: University of Florida Press, 1974), 278, 341; Edward C. Williamson, *Florida Politics in the Gilded Age, 1877-1893* (Gainesville: University of Florida Press, 1976), 37, 62, 91, 96, 113, 123, 131-32.

23 New York *Freeman*, April 11, 1885; Jacksonville *Florida Daily Times*, July 7, 1882; Jacksonville *Evening Telegram*, October 6, 1891; Jacksonville *Florida Times-Union*, June 20, 1889.

24 The Savannah *Daily Advertiser*, April 28, 1872; Tallahassee *Weekly Floridian*, March 26, 1872; Philadelphia *Christian Recorder*, July 29, 1871. On Florida's political life and the AME church's role in it during the early 1870s, see Canter Brown, Jr., *Ossian Bingley Hart, Florida's Loyalist Reconstruction Governor* (Baton Rouge: Louisiana State University Press, 1997), 223-50; Brown, *Florida's Black Public Officials*, 15-42, 110, 123; Rivers and Brown, *Laborers in the Vineyard of the Lord*, 62-100.

25 Pensacola *Republican*, July 4, 1874. For the life and times of Josiah T. Walls, see Klingman, *Josiah Walls*; Joe M. Richardson, *The Negro in the Reconstruction of Florida, 1865-1877* (Tallahassee: Florida State University Press, 1965; reprint ed., Tampa: Trend House, 1973); Jerrell H. Shofner, "Reconstruction and Renewal, 1865-1877" in *The New History of Florida*, ed. by Michael Gannon (Gainesville: University Press of Florida, 1996), 249-65.

26 Jacksonville *Florida Union*, April 7, 1874; Pensacola *Republican*; Jacksonville *Tri-Weekly Florida Union*, June 18, 1874.

27 Gainesville *Times*, October 5, 1876; Washington (D.C.) *Bee*, April 7, 1883; New York *Globe*, April 5, May 26, June 2, July 26, August 9, 1883.

28 Tallahassee *Weekly Floridian*, July 18, 1876; Brown, *Ossian Bingley Hart*, 294-300.

29 Tallahassee *Weekly Floridian*, August 8, October 10, 1876; Beatty, "John Willis Menard," 126-27; Klingman, *Josiah Walls*, 111.

30 Tampa *Guardian*, January 10, 1880.

31 Tallahassee *Weekly Floridian*, June 19, 1877.

32 See New York *Globe*, June 2, 1883; Hine, Hine, and Harrold, *African-American Odyssey*, 345.

33 Peter D. Klingman, *Neither Dies Nor Surrenders: A History of the Republican Party of Florida, 1867-1970* (Gainesville: University of Florida Press, 1984), 85; Shofner, "Florida," 92-93; Philadelphia *Christian Recorder*, July 13, 1882; New York *Globe*, May 31, 1884.

34 Jacksonville *Florida Times-Union*, February 7, 1884.

35 Tallahassee *Weekly Floridian*, July 4, 1882; New York *Globe*, April 21, 1883.

36 New York *Globe*, June 21, 1884; Williamson, *Florida Politics in the Gilded Age*, 131-32; New York *Freeman*, April 3, July 24, 1886; Shofner, "Florida," 94. See also Edward C. Williamson, "Independentism: A Challenge to the Florida Democracy of 1884," *Florida Historical Quarterly* 27 (October 1948), 131-56; Jacksonville *Florida Union*, August 18, 1882; Savannah *Weekly Echo*, August 26, 1883.

37 New York *Freeman*, May 26, June 18, 25, July 16, August 27, September 24, 1887; New York *Age*, January 12, November 23, 1889; Detroit *Plain Dealer*, September 20, 1889.

38 Madison *Recorder*, January 11, 1889.

39 New York *Freeman*, August 28, 1886. For an account of the temperance movement among blacks in the AME Church in Florida, see Rivers and Brown, *Laborers in the Vineyard of the Lord*, 77, 91, 103-104, 106-107, 136, 143, 146, 177.

40 New York *Age*, November 11, 1889; Philadelphia *Christian Recorder*, October 17, 1889; *Tampa Journal*, March 28, September 12, 1889.

41 Pensacola *Daily News*, October 13, 1893; Beatty, "John Willis Menard," 141.

42 Washington (D.C.) *Colored American*, September 17, 1898; Pensacola *Daily News*, October 13, 1893. See also Joan R. Sherman, *Invisible Poets: Afro-Americans of the Nineteenth Century* (Urbana: University of Illinois Press, 1974), 97-102; Richardson, *Negro in the Reconstruction of Florida*; Beatty, "John Willis Menard," 143.

John Willis Menard.

The Poetry of John Willis Menard:
Rediscovering an American Voice & Vision

John Willis Menard moved to Jacksonville, Florida, with his family in 1871. Just thirty-three years old when he arrived at this bustling town not far removed from its frontier origins, he brought with him an extraordinary range of experiences, including wilderness farming, political work in the nation's capital, and a talent for writing and politics that soon would establish him as a pioneering journalist, civil rights leader, editor, and poet. As noted in the preceding essay, his skills as an author and editor were already well honed. He had attained influence and recognition as a journalist and editor-publisher with the *Radical Standard* in New Orleans, and he had attracted national praise for his skillful oratory as the first African American to address Congress. Less widely recognized, however, were his range and accomplishments as a poet. This aspect of his work obviously ranked high in importance to him. He had composed lines to preserve and reflect upon personal and professional experiences after leaving college. He would continue to write steadily during his years in Jacksonville and Key West. When *Lays in Summer Lands* was published in 1879, its title and contents reflected almost a full decade of significant experience in the Sunshine State. Today his long-neglected poetry is a substantial body of work with an authentic literary voice and vision. It is a uniquely American poetry written at a time when the nation still was searching for its literary voice; and it is a distinctly Floridian poetry penned at a time when the state was presumed to have no literary culture.

The significance of poetry in Menard's time should not be underestimated. Walt Whitman had written in his 1855 Preface to *Leaves of Grass*: "The Americans of all nations at any time upon the earth have probably the fullest poetical nature. The United States themselves are essentially the greatest poem."[1] Menard's poetry is fully American in this best sense. While the standard surveys of literature look to New England for the emergence of the American voice, explaining how colonial writers carved a new literature from British traditions, they have overlooked an important geography, sensibility, and achievement in the greater Louisiana territory. There Menard composed poetry in an educated language one might call "frontier fusion," blending African, French, Caribbean, and Native American elements to shape poems that are in some ways more "American" than those of the New Englanders. The distinct voice rings out clearly in his poetry. Its verse weds the vernacular with the unmistakable contours of a classical education, passion with religion, sensitivity with rugged masculinity, humor with anger, and pride with humility. Moreover, it is a poetry of scrappy politics and dissent.

Menard exemplifies a sensibility in some ways sympathetic to the transcendentalism and self-reliance of Emerson and Thoreau, but for him there remains a deep respect for collective identity, social institutions, and political process that can unite and empower black Americans as "we the people." In sensibility and tone there is from time to time a hint of a grassroots John Greenleaf Whittier, but Whittier is aristocratic and distantly erudite by comparison, and all of these authors were about thirty years his senior—the prior generation to Menard. In age alone perhaps he is closest to Emily Dickinson, who was born in 1830, but Dickinson's habits of reclusive solitude and isolation stand in dramatic contrast to Menard's public and political disposition. One might classify him with the emerging regionalists, such as Mark Twain, Bret Harte, and Joel Chandler Harris, yet despite some similarities Menard claims a distinct position for himself. He is a Southern regionalist with an international sensibility, a Florida writer aiming to reach an American audience, a black writer speaking for the depth and integrity of his race and for his complex individuality as a human being.

Menard's early influences offer a context for understanding the evolution of his voice. He spent the first 18 years of his life on a farm in Kaskaskia, Illinois. The town had taken its name from the indigenous Kaskaskia Indians. It stood on the western edge of the state, south of St. Louis at a bend in the Mississippi River near the modern city of Chester and had served as the territorial capital and later as first state capital of Illinois. Menard eventually would wander far from this place, but its importance for him can be seen in the central, pivotal poem in his book, "A Visit to My Native Home." In it, he affirms that his experiences there "will remain the bright dream" against which the rest of his life is measured and contrasted.

Menard's immediate family boasted a French Creole background. Though the French population of Illinois was never large, the state traces its modern history from 1673 when French explorers Louis Joliet and Father Jacques Marquette travelled southward from Canada along the Mississippi and Illinois Rivers. Again in 1682 Frenchman Robert Cavelier de La Salle explored the area from the south and called the entire region Louisiana. The French flag flew over the territory until the 1762 Treaty of Fontainebleau between France and Great Britain, when all French possessions east of the Mississippi, excepting New Orleans, were turned over to the British. In 1765 British soldiers defeated the most tenacious remaining French ally Native American chief Pontiac, thereby gaining physical control of the territory. Nonetheless, the families of French settlers remained important. The Menard family was sufficiently prominent to have produced John Willis's white grandfather Pierre, the first Lieutenant-Governor of Illinois, and to have bestowed its family name on Menard counties in Illinois and Texas. The family could trace its lineage north to Quebec and south to New Orleans and Texas.

Willis Menard clearly showed sufficient intellectual and creative promise as a youth to be sent to college preparatory school in Sparta, Illinois. At twenty-one, he entered Iberia College (later called Ohio Central College), traditionally a black institution under the Synod of the Free Presbyterian Church of the United States of America.[2] How much college Menard completed remains unclear, but his poetry evidences a strong education, including wide knowledge of the classics, history, and composition skills. Shortly after leaving school, he won appointment as the first black clerk in the U.S. Department of the Interior in Washington, D.C.[3]

During the future poet's youth, slavery loomed as a major issue in Illinois, with abolitionist sentiment burning in the northern part of the state and pro-slavery stalwarts dominating in the southern part—including at Kaskaskia. The Illinois General Assembly had enacted oppressive "black laws" restricting the rights of blacks in 1853. Abraham Lincoln's challenge of incumbent United States senator Stephen A. Douglas in 1858 resulted in the famous Lincoln-Douglas debates in which Lincoln argued the moral and legal injustice of slavery on the basis of its denying blacks the right to "life, liberty and the pursuit of happiness." Whether Menard attended any of these debates is not known, but given the political prominence and activism of the Menard family in Illinois, quite possibly he did. In any case, he participated in the continuing and extended debate within the wider community. Shortly after this, to cite an example, Menard published his first major piece of writing, *An Address to the Free Colored People of Illinois*. In it he aligned himself with American patriots in language reminiscent of the Declaration of Independence: "The recent enactments of Missouri, Arkansas, Mississippi, Alabama, Tennessee and Kentucky are too severe for any free people to endure," he wrote.

"Countrymen! Arise! . . . Have we not petitioned repeatedly? Did we get our rights? No! They have answered us only by repeated acts of injustice and usurpation." For his part, Menard's call for independence urges blacks to leave the United States altogether to establish their own nation. It also appeals to what is highest and most noble, to show that his countrymen are not "chattels" but "men of stability, of firmness, and of confirmed virtue."[4] Impressively articulate, idealis-

Menard's first publication.

tic, and impassioned, the essay did not fall upon deaf ears. Among others who noticed this young man were leaders in a new administration then changing politics in Washington, D.C.

The year was 1862, an exciting and inspiring time to be in the nation's capital. The Civil War brought purpose and intensity to government as the young nation struggled to assert a more fundamental and universal definition of freedom and civil rights. Menard arrived just months after a family acquaintance and virtual neighbor in rural Illinois, Abraham Lincoln, had been inaugurated as the sixteenth President. (Lincoln had settled in Menard County, in New Salem, Illinois, in 1831 and had worked there as storekeeper, postmaster, surveyor, and, eventually, lawyer). Correspondence in the Lincoln Papers Collection at the Library of Congress includes letters from Peter Menard to Lincoln, a fact that highlights the family connection.[5] Menard's political ideals—and to some extent his political, oratorical, and editorial styles—were shaped by Lincoln and the Republican party that he led with such extraordinary words and vision. Given the context of Menard's early professional and political work in Washington, he naturally begins his book of poems with lines written to honor his hero in "To President Lincoln."

Little is known about Menard's day-to-day responsibilities at the Interior department, but at that time this agency played a significant role in both national and territorial affairs. In addition to issues related to territorial administration and exploration, Native American treaties, and homesteading, the department had been drawn into war-related discussions over slavery. Specifically, several proposals addressed the possibility of relocating slaves, who had been transported to the United States from many parts of the world, to a designated colonial homeland outside U.S. borders. Menard publicly advocated independence and self-reliance as among his highest principles. In this, his views echo Emerson (whose essay "Self-Reliance" was published first in 1841, when Menard was ten) and express a distinctly American idealism. When an Englishman offered the government land in the Central American country of Belize (at that time called

British Honduras) to form, in effect, an African American state. The Commissioner of Emigration chose Menard to visit there and to report on its potential. So far as we know, this constituted Menard's first international trip, and it marked the beginning of travels that familiarized him with countries sharing access to the Gulf of Mexico—a cluster of primarily Spanish-, English-, and French-speaking lands steeped in rich black and colonial cultures. These travels eventually added significantly to his literary sensibility, molding him as the first Florida writer to embrace these Caribbean and colonial neighbors. His experiences of their cultures certainly would figure significantly in his life and writing when he later settled in the state. At the time, Menard returned to Washington. His report, which was published, prompted no action.[6]

A more immediate crisis claimed the nation's attention. In the Interior department in Washington, Menard experienced the war, helping to cope with its losses and its aftermath. He was there when Lincoln was assassinated on April 14, 1865, and he felt the loss profoundly. Later that year he left the city, accepting an appointment as Inspector of Customs in New Orleans—a significant post, given the importance of New Orleans as a major U.S. port. Subsequently, he also served as Commissioner of Streets. In addition to these important positions, he published a newspaper there called *The Free South*, establishing a good reputation as an editor and journalist. Eventually he changed the paper's name to *The Radical Standard*, giving it a more prominent political profile. On November 3, 1868, he contested a special election held in Lousiana's Second Congressional District to fill a vacancy due to the death of Congressman James Mann. Menard received 5,104 votes to 2,833 for his opponent, Caleb S. Hunt. Hunt challenged the election. As you have read in the preceding essay, when Menard attempted to take his seat in Congress, his fellow Republicans denied him the seat.[7]

Menard seems to have returned to New Orleans to regroup and reconsider, for with this matter decided in such an unsatisfactory and unfair manner—and without political recourse to fight it—he must have felt a fresh start was necessary. Little more than two years later, in 1871, he moved to Jacksonville, where he received an appointment with the post office.

In Florida, the disappointed politician also returned to journalism. First, he wrote for and helped edit the *Florida Sun* (sometimes called the *Jacksonville Sun*), soon winning recognition as a community leader there. As historians Rivers and Brown have explained, within two years he was elected to a term in the Florida legislature (1873-1875), after which he accepted appointment as deputy collector of Internal Revenue at Jacksonville. Disheartened by the Republican political machine in the state and what he considered to be white "bossism" within the state party, he resigned the appointment within a relatively short time, though he remained active in the national party and served as a delegate to the national Republican convention that nominated Rutherford B. Hayes in 1876. During that year he opposed Republican Florida governor Marcellus L. Stearns's candidacy while he worked energetically for Hayes on the national ticket. In this he united with Josiah Walls, the state's other influential black journalist and editor. Both men must have been pleased when Hayes won

Jacksonville was an important port town when Menard arrived.

while Democrat George F. Drew achieved election as governor. Drew showed his appreciation by appointing Menard as a justice of the peace in Duval County.

Over the next two years in Jacksonville, Menard concentrated on writing and publishing. He turned out intelligent and insightful editorials for his newspaper, sometimes spoke at meetings and political events. State and national papers often quoted him. His high professional standards and astute commentary inspired respect and emulation. During this time he also prepared the final manuscript for *Lays in Summer Lands*. Individual poems appeared in newspapers, and a small national advertising campaign helped attract attention. Menard's public appearances by 1879 thus had become literary as well as political events.

This ad that appeared in the Washington, D.C. People's Advocate on September 27, 1879, announced "The Literary Event of the Season."

In the early 1880s an appointment as U.S. Customs Inspector prompted Menard to relocate for a time to Key West, where in 1882 he purchased a newspaper, the *Island City News* (also published as the Key West *News*), and published it successfully there for several years before relocating it back to Jacksonville in 1885 to become something of a family business. The paper's name was changed to *The Southern Leader*, and he hoped to establish it as a major editorial presence throughout the South in partnership with his son, Willis, and later with the added assistance of his talented son-in-law, Thomas Van Renssalaer Gibbs. Unfortunately, a serious outbreak of yellow fever prompted him to suspend publication, and in the summer of 1889 Menard made a final move, back to Washington, D.C.,

The nameplate of Key West's Island City News.

where he accepted a position in the census office, hoping also to continue working as an editor and publisher, this time aiming for a national audience under the masthead of a new monthly magazine he called the *National Afro-American*. He never fully succeeded, however, before failing health led to his death on October 8, 1893.

The events of Menard's life suggest continuing and evolving relevance for the poetry. Through the verses of *Lays in Summer Lands* he plunges us into the midst of his early experiences in Illinois and Washington with the opening poem to Abraham Lincoln. In that poem he stakes out the scale and range of his work. From triumphant idealism to heartfelt loss and from public persona to intimate personal expression, this is a volume filled with hopes and fears, its author daring to walk shoulder to shoulder with Lincoln, Grant, and other national leaders. One could call this "namedropping" but for the fact that the poems are filled with varied names, familiar and unknown: "For M.E.T.," "A Lady," "My Sister," or "To Madame Selika." These are poems for the people he lived and worked among—for his race, for its admirable and inspiring women, for ordinary citizens, and for leaders of the sort he himself aspired to be—capable of moving his compatriots toward the promise of equality with stirring and inspiring words.

In his "Preface" to the first edition F. G. Barbadoes points to an animating principle for Menard: the Civil War brought the benefits of freedom, the right to vote, and the right to hold office. These freedoms also carried responsibilities to act on behalf of lofty purpose for the common good, to exercise the right to vote with intelligence and diligence, and to hold public office as a trust for true public service and in a manner that history would regard favorably.

"Our race can only succeed in winning a place in history by culti-
vating a pride of race though a high order of character and educa-
tion," Barbadoes wrote, "for a race will be remembered only by its
deeds, and not by its condition and numbers."[8]

Menard's poem to Lincoln celebrates just such a leader, and
it serves as an invocation of praise for the power of the word.
Each of the first four stanzas begins with the word, and three of
the four repeat the same phrase, "Thou hast spoken!" The text
resonates with the rolling cadences of the King James Bible. Be-
hind the force of law and justice is the preacher reminding us
that "in the beginning was the word." And that emancipation
had its roots in words, from the Declaration of Independence,
the Constitution, and the Bill of Rights, through the Lincoln-
Douglas debates to the White House and what later came to be
called its "bully pulpit." Menard drives home the point in the
fourth stanza when he declares that Lincoln's name, itself a word,
"shall glow/Forever on Columbia's altar." The very District of
Columbia, to draw a narrow circle, becomes a sanctuary com-
plete with altar. Menard completes the poem acknowledging a
great price for freedom in the sacrifices and losses of the war,
and in the loss of Lincoln's life. That loss is counterbalanced at
the end of the poem through a kind of transfiguration in which
Lincoln joins a heavenly band of Patriots in immortality.

Menard follows the opening poem with "Grant's First Elec-
tion." Here, however, the military general and president take back
seat to an invocation of the muse that echoes a convention of
classical literature: "Once more, O harp! let me gentle touch/
The thrilling numbers soft and sweet." Again, the theme is lib-
erty, and the poem contains a deft couplet illustrative of Menard's
talents: "For Heaven gave/No man a slave." The tight, direct
wording and skillful rhyme reinforce with intelligence and wit
the argument's content. Menard's own talents and independence
of thought reinforce the idea that individuals should not be judged
by accident of birth or skin color. The two opening poems estab-
lish Menard as a complex and sophisticated man with a grasp of
politics, history, literature, society, education, and belief. These

works are not mere superficial exercises in rhyme and meter: they are authentic poems with depths of thought and feeling.

Interestingly they play against one another: the poem to the lawyer president and one to the soldier president. In the first there is praise and celebration for Lincoln's words that change the country; in the second the poet asks that he might find the words to praise Grant, the soldier and the man of action or deeds rather than of word and vision. But Menard has not yet finished the introductory section of his work. The third poem that completes his "opening" is "The Wife's Invocation." Here a poem that is personal and intimate supplants the classical invocation of the muse, presenting through the individual joining of husband and wife the problem of unity and separation—the ultimate desire for and triumph of unity. "Love me, leave me not" could be the North's plea to the secessionist South, but here the sacred union worthy of preservation is intimate and transcendent: "We have kiss'd and truly given/Vows before the sacred shrine;/ and we're one on earth—in Heaven—/You are mine and I am thine."

Menard has arranged a brilliant opening for the volume. In these first three poems he demonstrates an ability to summon the personal to universal ends. Lincoln and Grant are public, historic figures, but they also stand in personal relationship to him. His relationship with his wife in the third poem could be merely confessional, but in his hands the poem gains a more universal standing. It becomes in fact another statement of both thought and feeling on behalf of preserving the union—and a bedrock conviction that there *is* transcendent union beyond any temporary division: "Soon from earth we'll pass away; But we'll meet, where here we sever,/In a brighter land of day." History, equality, liberty, love, and unity remain important themes throughout the poems in this collection.

Another secret this rich book holds is its discovery of many ways to root the poems in the particularity of place. They are "lays in summer lands," as they touch upon particular stories, people, and geographies. Florida is the "summer land" *par excellence*, but Menard is a citizen of an extended location that mirrors Florida's modern identity as a state in touch with its Caribbean neighbors. Jamaica, Honduras, Belize, and Cuba are mentioned specifically—and these are the places that were most significant for Menard personally—but by implication he embraces others as well. His French heritage allied his sympathies with French-colonial Caribbean islanders; his black heritage and his fervent dedication to liberty and equality wed his spirit with the Cubans.

Cuban liberty stood as a cause close to his heart, one that gained immediacy from Florida's proximity to the island and because of the considerable Key West population of Cuban cigar workers. Menard's "Stanzas on Cuba" issues a fervent cry for U.S. intervention to "reach out" to end servitude in Cuba and the Western hemisphere. As he insists, "Come war or peace, that island must be free." As becomes clear, Menard's grasp of the issues of freedom ranged far beyond individual, racial, or national interests. He asserts an international claim for the principles animating the French and American Revolutions—and the Civil War. The "Patriot" he imagines and describes is an international figure dedicated to liberty and equality. Menard's ability to cast the issue beyond American borders and his placing of the "Patriot's band" in the very first poem of his collection as part of a "bright, celestial land" shows his insistence on the transcendent importance of liberty without borders. He returns to drive the point home in his later poem "Free Cuba" in which he asserts that the march "for equal rights" must continue, since "God makes man free when he for freedom fights." Here he praises Cuban independence while urging that the fight continue: "now let Brazil awake/From her vile bondage, and her fetters break!"

The final line of "Stanzas on Cuba" offers a particularly interesting example of innovative use of American vernacular idioms combined with sophisticated word play. Menard concludes with surprising freedom. This effect emerges as more pronounced because the poem begins with more conventionally formal cadence, syntax, and poetic conventions, such as the formal personification of the spirit of liberty in the first line of the second stanza. There Menard urges, "Reach out, Columbia! thy powerful hand." His final line seems almost out of place in its freedom. The poem's shortest line, it is the most important: "The jig is up, all hail the jubalee!" The phrasing begins with a casual, slang expression, and "jig" is an especially interesting and apt word choice because of connotations on multiple levels. As a slang expression "the jig is up" means that the game is over, that a scheme is exposed and the day of reckoning has arrived. But "jig" also carries connotations of a lively dance to someone else's fiddling—as in an Irish jig—or more traditionally hearkening back to its French origins as "gigue," a French word for fiddle and a seventeenth-century dance. "Jubilee" is a word with a popular meaning of celebration or a day of great joy. In the Old Testament the Jubilee year was one in which all seized lands had to be returned, and slaves set free. This allusion casts the American slave experience into a biblical perspective and reminds the reader of the Old Testament tribe of God's chosen people forced into bondage. But Menard renders "jubilee" with an "a," an uncharacteristic but intriguing spelling error. Again, Menard rewards close and thoughtful reading. On closer look "Jubalee" shows Menard taking skillful liberty with language in this poem about freedom. "Juba" is a word from African American folklore that designates a ghost or spirit and also connotes an African American dance, a word some thought derived from rhythmic nonsense syllables, "juba, juba," used in refrains of black folksongs and spirituals. Menard uses it as a pivotal word of transformation, changing a deceptive "jig" danced to someone else's tune into a triumphant African American dance of "juba," in a distinctly black American language of jubilation that mirrors biblical Jubilee.[9]

If this were the only example of free and playful use of American idioms and folk traditions, there would be less reason to dwell upon it. But careful reading reveals a fascinating pattern of similar poetic liberties and innovations. Folk motifs also find their ways into poems through Caribbean island tales, as in "Estella" and "The Murdered Bride." Even the book's title resonates with overtones drawn from ordinary American usage and allusion to the French poetic *lais* of the Middle Ages that celebrated courtly love and fairy kingdoms in short lyrical and narrative verse. Layers of meaning underlie his title, for the book in one sense conveys the "lay of the land" politically and geographically; yet simultaneously in the tradition of the medieval *lai* it draws in ideals of courtly love and analogies to Arthurian legend—a vanished Camelot in which Lincoln might have presided over a Reconstruction "round table" with Menard as one of his knights. As elsewhere, especially when he touches on matters of great beauty, delicacy, or feeling, Menard uses positive folkloric and courtly connotations of the word "fairy." The word appears frequently, and the author applies it using American and French overtones. He presents a delicate, diminutive, helpful "fairy," different from the troubling Germanic creatures that are part demon, but rather leaning toward the benevolent domestic folktales in the French traditions collected and preserved in the seventeenth century by Charles Perrault in *Histoires ou contes du temps passé*.[10]

One key use of "fairy" occurs in "Florida," which describes the primary "summer land" of the book's title. In this poem the state is personified as a "sweet ocean goddess" and addressed using the literary figure of speech called *apostrophe*. "Thou art a fairy land," Menard writes, in this case not invoking diminutive images such as those found in Andrew Lang's fairy books, but conjuring a fair land of magical beauty "and balmy sky,/Where summer reigns and flowers never die." It bursts full of hope for a state at last rid of slavery: "Thy chains have fallen, and ended is thy night." Menard proves uncannily prescient as he predicts that the state will "lure from every clime, from every land,/Uncounted thousands to thy shores of sand." His imagination for the future remains far more idealistic than the commercial Disney "Magic Kingdom" that has come to pass, complete with Disney's fairy "Tinker Bell," but no doubt exists that his decision to characterize the state as a "fairy land" connotes a special, mythic quality. An elevated term, it designates a step halfway between the earthly and divine. The poem's first line speaks of the personified Florida as "divinely fair and free." But by not applying conventionally religious language and moving instead toward "fairy land,"

Menard affirms that certain physical realities resonate with secular enchantment. In a sense, the term functions as a fusion of classical sensibility which could have found its analogs in figures from classical mythology, and the romantic sensibility, which soon finds voice in landmark American fantasy (L. Frank Baum published *The Wonderful Wizard of Oz* about twenty years later in 1900).

The word "fairy" appears more than a dozen times in this collection, and "fair," together with variations, can be found upward of two dozen. The magical aspects often associate with feelings engendered by women and children and specific places that are emotionally charged. In context it evokes beauty and idealism partaking in the transfiguring quality of dream. Glimpsing it refreshes one's vision and uplifts one's spirits. Moreover, it embraces the morality of "fairness" in the best sense, and thus seems appropriate for an author whose political and editorial efforts were directed toward achieving fair treatment for all persons. He imagines an end to discrimination in the "fair sunny South" in "Grant's First Election." In another important Florida poem, "Under the Pine and Palm," he experiences "fair Nature in her best array" and imagines an interracial marriage of equals within the state's "fairy borders." The majestic St. Johns River is a "fairy stream." Yet the harsh violations recounted in "The Solid South," and "The Negro's Lament," two of his strongest and darkest poems, undercut the reality of fairness that he glimpses, and the promise he finds in the natural world.

The voice that emerges is that of a complex poet who writes honestly of both the dreams and realities of his life. In this he practices what critics often mention as a distinctively American style—the writing of "songs of myself," a universal poetry the poet sings from his own most personal experience. Whitman celebrates the workers and soldiers he encounters, the Civil War experience, the physical experience of his own body moving through the world, and the American scene and geography. Menard writes poems on many of these same subjects, but his experience includes contact with the politics and politicians of his time, the realities of racial prejudice, and a wide geographic experience that includes the Caribbean and the "fair South."

Near the center of his book he places his poem "A Visit To My Native Home." His return to Illinois is described in terms that seem reminiscent of the environment associated with "Honest Abe":

> Here is the rustic house of logs,
>   Hewn broad with axe and line;
> And steers, and cows, and mules, and dogs,
>   And restless, nosing swine!
>
> And down below the cotton wood,
>   The dear old river sweeps;
> While on its bank in solitude
>   The flowing willow weeps.

The frontier scene serves as an idyllic foil to the more urban frontier and tropical environment of Florida. Now he celebrates Florida as "sunny land of the orange" in marked contrast to the Illinois farmer dependent on "ripening wheat and corn," but these geographies and agricultures ring true. The "dear old river" he returns to is the Mississippi that ran past Kaskaskia and marked his home at New Orleans. Yet in Florida he finds an analog in the St. Johns a "fairy stream" with "sweet enchantment" holding him there. Even though it cannot match the Mississippi for size or commercial importance, the river becomes his locus of "grandeur" as he affirms his Florida home: "Your grandeur will forever seem/The day-dream of my life!" It is an active, present echo of the retrospective treatment of the Mississippi: "Your ties and memories will remain/The bright dream of my days!" There is a certain conflation or convergence of these images. The operative river in current play is the lesser known St. Johns. He brings the past to bear upon the present, but does not trade off one for the other . . . nor make one lesser and the other greater. There is a fairness in the equal claim.

The poems gather weight as their author speaks honestly from his own experience, accepting and celebrating life as it unfolds its present and future possibilities. The scope of style and vision is impressive as much for the small passing moments as for large vistas and great rivers. "Seven Hours at Live Oak!" combines an ironic tone and an ability to laugh at himself while painting a scene that will ring true to most Floridians. Menard injects comic relief as he strikes a wonderfully dramatic posture "Amid boxcars and logs,/And the music of the frogs" virtually in the middle of nowhere "waiting in the cold and rain/For the Savannah train!" Here is a perfect little dramatic monologue as a grand gentleman fusses about the inconvenience. With his tongue firmly in his cheek, Menard inserts a perfect incongruity as the speaker in the poem complains, "Ye gods of Rome and Greece,/When shall this waiting cease." Our awareness of all the greatness of the classical world converges in this rainy, bug-infested wait in the Florida backwoods for the latest technology (the train) to take him away. Heartbreaking poignancy lies behind the humor as we pause to think of Menard's life journey, of his suffering the unfairness and racism that locked him out of Congress and distanced him from the heartbeat of the politics of freedom. We can smile with him at his staged rage waiting for the train. But once we have read the book and can experience this poem in the light of a second reading, when we contemplate this great man stranded on the outskirts of civilization, we inevitably recall the haunting opening lines of "The Negro's Lament"—"How long, O God! how long must I remain/Worse than an alien in my native land?"

Menard translates personal life experiences for universal purposes throughout the book. The technique is perhaps most effective, and at the same time most elusive, in the poems about

Live Oak, Florida, served as a railroad hub for Jacksonville and other cities. This change bill offers a visual memento of Menard's memorable wait.

women. Some critics have read these as the semi-autobiographi-
cal celebrations of a womanizer . . . and, indeed, Menard does seem
to wrestle with attractions to more than one woman. Yet many of
the poems are clearly written to those closest to him, first to his
future wife, then to his wife and to his daughters. Again, the range
of the work impresses with flirtation, wit, admiration, friendship,
romance, passion, and heartbreak. "A Glance," for example, is a
deft and adept short poem about having one's heart swept up in a
moment. Its position in the manuscript, immediately following
"Sabbath Eve Musings" heightens the effect. Religion weaves its
way throughout the book; in this flirtatious little poem, the ob-
ject of affection is "half of earth and half of heaven." Add to this
comment the prior poem on the eve of the Sabbath the fact that
the maiden's name is Mary, and the author compounds the blend
of earth and heaven in a manner that again recalls the best tradi-
tions of courtly poetry. The second stanza closes the poem with a
skillfully turned conceit, nearly metaphysical in its wit: "And she
who chains a wild bird's wing,/Must start not if her captive sing!"
One way of paraphrasing this is that the maiden who has
capitivated this free spirit should not be surprised if he bursts into
song—or poetry—in his cage. Is this an admission that the poet has
an eye for the ladies and can be easily distracted from loyalties to
wife and home? Is this a charming domestic moment as a father's
heart is captivated by his daughter Mary?

Because so much remains to be discovered regarding the facts
of Menard's life, unraveling the emotions and relationships in
the poems inspired by women poses difficulties. Yet many poems
address them, and the book is dedicated to a female friend: "To
Mrs. Emma V. Montgomery, my faithful critic and friend of past
years."[11] It seems far less important to solve biographical riddles
in these poems than to appreciate the way they paint closely ob-
served nuances of relationships. As in the overall issues of sla-
very and freedom, the ties that bind us or enslave us to loved
ones and friends can be virtually impossible to understand and
sometimes difficult to bear. Nonetheless, Menard clearly writes
about and celebrates the people to whom he is emotionally clos-

Willis T. Menard.   *T. V. Gibbs.*

est. Whatever women may have turned his head (and there seems
to be a moment when his wife takes his daughters and leaves
him, perhaps because of an alleged affair or perhaps simply to
visit her family in Jamaica). Whatever the cause, the highly charged
poem with its chant-like call-and-response coda that pleas "come
back to me" is one of his most successful.

In the end of a volume that develops both thematically and
roughly chronologically from first to last, the poet concludes by
celebrating education—his hope for lifting black and white alike
beyond treason and prejudice. Biography and poetic vision meld
in the marriage of his daughter Alice to Thomas Van Renssalaer
Gibbs. Menard must have taken great pride in this union, for
the Gibbs name already reflected high ideals, education, and po-
litical progress in Florida. His son-in-law became a partner in the
printing and journalistic enterprises Menard and his son Willis
managed with their influential *Southern Leader.* Soon Gibbs la-
bored in Tallahassee in the midst of politics, while working as
the Tallahassee Normal School's assistant principal. Here he
would shape the state's first great black institution of higher edu-
cation when he introduced the legislation creating the State
Normal College for Colored Students (later Florida Agricultural
and Mechanical University). As the book draws to a close, "Our

J. WILLIS MENARD.   WILLIS T. MENARD.

THE SOUTHERN LEADER,

Menard & Son, Editors and Proprietors.
OFFICE, COR. PINE & ADAMS STREETS.

Jacksonville, Fla., _____, 188__

Stationery for The Southern Leader.

District School Teachers" offers a tribute to the teachers (and future teachers) of Florida, and an affirmation of his son-in-law's work in education.

And it is through education that the final poem in the book constructs a fitting symmetry to balance the opening invocations of the muse—those three first poems evoking politics, warfare, and love in the poems to Lincoln, Grant, and wife—for his ending repeats the poetical convention of a poetic *envoi* that takes leave of the reader and sends the book out on its way into the world. Menard does this with appropriate individuality. In calling it "Adieu," he punctuates his French-American heritage. By entrusting his mind and heart to the words of his book he takes a leap of faith that well-educated future generations will be able to read and understand it. He sets it free. The ending is a quiet, personal parallel to the celebration of Lincoln's emancipation proclamation. How poetically appropriate it is that the marriage union of his daughter with Florida's wellspring educator could embody the possibility of a "more perfect union" than he has witnessed in his poems of struggle.

It has taken a long time for readers to fulfill Menard's hopes— nearly one hundred and twenty-five years since first publication. His injunction to "go, gentle book" almost was lost to current generations. But today his words can be read and understood anew, for we are at last on the verge of producing better educated generations of all races and ethnicities who can comprehend and respond to his message. This is a remarkable, honest book that is at once a "song of myself" and a "song of America." Menard has written a call to practice justice, union, and communion—in the words of Allen Ginsberg, also a disciple of Whitman, "the absolute heart of the poem of life butchered out of their own bodies good to eat a thousand years."[12]

A moonlight view of Jacksonville in the 1880s.

Notes

1 Sculley Bradley, Richmond Croom Beatty, et. al., *The American Tradition in Literature* (New York: Grosset & Dunlap, 1974), 1709.

2 Located in a two-story brick building, the school was first a high school operated by Rev. J. B. Blaney and later became a ladies' seminary under the direction of Miss Mary J. Haft. The Free Presbyterian synod obtained a charter from the Legislature of Ohio to grant it college powers in 1854 and it became Iberia College, open to all classes "without restriction of sex, race, or color." After the Civil War it passed to the United Presbyterian Presbytery of Mansfield, Ohio, and changed its named to Ohio Central in 1875. See *History of Morrow County and Ohio* (Chicago: O. L. Baskin, 1880) 407-409.

3 Edith Menard, "John Willis Menard, First Negro Elected to the U.S. Congress, First Negro to Speak in the U.S. Congress," *Negro History Bulletin* 18 (December 1964), 53.

4 John Willis Menard, *An Address to the Free Colored People of Illinois* (Randolph County, Illinois: n.p., [c. 1860]), 1-2.

5 Peter Menard to Abraham Lincoln, April 4, 1849, and P. Menard to Abraham Lincoln, April 15, 1849. Abraham Lincoln Papers at the Library of Congress. Transcribed and annotated by the Lincoln Studies Center, Knox College, Galesburg, Illinois.

6 Edith Menard 53.

7 Ibid.

8 In J. Willis Menard, *Lays in Summer Lands: Poems by J. Willis Menard* (Washington, D.C.: Enterprise Publishing Company, 1879), v.

9 William Allan Neilson, Thomas A. Knott, and Paul W. Carhart, eds., *Webster's New International Dictionary of the English Language: Second Edition, Unabridged* (Springfield, Mass.: G. & C. Merriam Company, 1948).

10 Bruce Murphy, ed., *Benét's Reader's Encyclopedia*, Fourth Edition (New York: HarperCollins, 1996).

11 The full dedication reads: "To Mrs. Emma V. Montgomery, My faithful critic and friend of past years, and with kind wishes for her future happiness and prosperity, this book is respectfully dedicated." *Lays in Summer Lands* iv.

12 Allen Ginsberg, *Howl and Other Poems*, (San Francisco, Calif.: City Lights Books, 1959), 16.

Index of Titles ❧

Index of First Lines 🔊

Index of Names and Subjects

Lincoln, Abraham, 3, 32, 83, 101,
126-28, 131-32, 138, 142
Lincoln-Douglas debates, 126, 132
Lincoln Papers, 127
Live Oak, Fla., 15, 84, 138
Logan, Rayford W., 87
Louisiana, 87, 104-108, 125. *See
also* New Orleans
lynchings, 114

M
Macon, Ga., x
"Magic Kingdom," 136
Mann, James, 104, 128
Marquette, Jacques, 125
Menard, Alice. *See* Alice Menard
Gibbs
Menard, Elizabeth, 104, 106, 141
Menard, Josephine, 27
Menard, Mary (Marie) Jeannette.
See Mary Menard Kinloch
Menard, John Willis: images of, ii,
viii, 105, 122; literary legacy of, ix-
x, 91; early life of, xi-xii, 103-104,
124-28; publications of, 103-104,
126-27; as a journalist and editor,
104, 106-107, 112-15, 129-31;
election of to U.S. Congress, viii-
ix, 104-105, 128; relocation of to
Florida, 106, 123, 128-29; political
career of in Florida, 107-110, 129-
30; attempts by to gain diplomatic
post, 110-11, 115; departure of
from Florida, 115, 130; death of,
115, 131; poetical works of
analyzed, 123-43 . *See also Lays in
Summer Lands*
Menard, Peter, *127*
Menard, Pierre, 125
Menard, Willis T., 106, 112, 130,
141
Menard County, Ill., 125, 127
Menard County, Tex., 125
Mississippi River, 125, 138
Montgomery, Emma V. 140
music, 28

N
National Afro-American (Washing-
ton, D.C., magazine), 115, 131
New Orleans, La., x-xii, 104, 106-
108, 125, 128-29, 138
New Salem, Ill., 127
New South (Jacksonville newspaper),
108
New York, N.Y., 100, 112-114
newspapers. *See* individual names

O
Ohio, 103
Ohio Central College. *See* Iberia
College
Orlando, Fla., 96

P
Payne, Daniel A., 85, 92-93, 95
Pensacola, Fla., 98, 108, 115
Perrault, Charles, 136
Philadelphia, Pa., 67
Phillips, Wendell, 66
*Pleasures and Other Miscellaneous
Poems*, 95
Poems on Miscellaneous Subjects,
93
*Poems on Various Subjects,
Religious and Moral*, 88, 92
Polk County, Fla., 100-101
Pontiac (Native American leader),
125
Potomac River, 70
Prohibition. *See* temperance
movement
Purvis, Robert, 66

Q
Quebec, 125

R
Radical Standard (New Orleans
newspaper), xii, 104, 123, 128
Randolph County, Ill., 103-104

Acknowledgments

THE EDITORS gratefully acknowledge the special assistance of James Cusick, Curator, P. K. Yonge Library of Florida History, University of Florida, Gainesville; Betty Jean Hubbard Rivers and Barbara Gray Brown, Tallahassee; Julienne H. Empric, Eckerd College, St. Petersburg, Florida; John T. Foster Jr. and Sarah Whitmer Foster, Department of Sociology and Criminal Justice, Florida A&M University, Tallahassee; Maurice O'Sullivan, Rollins College, Winter Park, Florida; Robert W. Saunders Sr. and the late Rowena Ferrell Brady, Tampa; Leland Hawes, *Tampa Tribune*; Margaret Nichols and Cheryl Rowland, Division of Rare and Manuscript Collections, Carl A. Kroch Library, Cornell University, Ithaca, New York; George Heerman, Illinois State Historical Library, Old State Capitol, Springfield, Illinois; the Ohio Historical Society; Denison Beach, Houghton Library of the Harvard College Library, Cambridge, Massachusetts; Eileen Brady, University of North Florida Library, Jacksonville; Emily Liska, Jacksonville Historical Society, Jacksonville; Glenn Emory, Jacksonville Public Library; Louise Hane and Jeanne Vince, Macdonald-Kelce Library, University of Tampa; Mary Jane Schenck, Department of English and Writing, University of Tampa; Clifton and Vendarae Lewis, Bartow, Florida; LaFrancine K. Burton, Lakeland; Marcia Dean Felts, Jacksonville; Willie Mae Ashley, Fernandina Beach; Althemese Barnes and John Riley House, Tallahassee; David Jackson Jr., Sylvester Cohen, and Titus Brown, Department of History and Political Science, Florida A&M University; Michael Woodward, Wallace Ward, Stacey Reese, Gregory Harris, and Angela Freeman, Tallahassee; Mary Kemp Davis and DeSilver Cohen, Department of English, Florida A&M University; Erma Ellis, Cairo, Georgia; Aubrey M. Perry, Department of Psychology, Florida A&M University; Walter L. Smith, Tampa; Roosevelt Wilson and Yanela Gordon, Tallahassee *Capital Outlook*; and Sean Donnelly of the University of Tampa Press.

About the Editors

LARRY EUGENE RIVERS is Distinguished Professor of History at Florida A&M University, Tallahassee. He authored the national award-winning work *Slavery in Florida: Territorial Days to Emancipation* and co-authored the landmark study *Laborers in the Vineyard of the Lord: The Beginnings of the AME Church in Florida, 1865-1895*. Among numerous prizes and honors that he has received are the Carter G. Woodson Prize of the Association for the Study of African American Life and History, the Certificate of Commendation of the American Association for State and Local History, the Outstanding Nonfiction Award of the Black Caucus of the American Library Association; and the Rembert Patrick Book Award of the Florida Historical Society. A native of Philadelphia, Pennsylvania, he resides in Tallahassee, Florida.

RICHARD MATHEWS is Dana Professor of English at the University of Tampa and Director of the University of Tampa Press. He is the author of two books of poetry, *Mummery* and *Numbery*, and his poems have appeared in periodicals and anthologies including *Lyric, Poet Lore, Berkeley Poetry Review, Southern Poetry Review*, and *A Geography of Poets*. As a literary critic he has written book-length studies of William Morris, J. R. R. Tolkien, Anthony Burgess, and Brian Aldiss and is co-editor of *Subtropical Speculations: An Anthology of Florida Science Fiction*. His book on fantasy as a literary genre, *Fantasy: The Liberation of Imagination*, is being reprinted in a new paperback edition by Routledge in 2002. He has lived in Florida since 1950.

CANTER BROWN JR. has taught at Florida A&M University and served as Historian in Residence at the Tampa Bay History Center. Among numerous other significant works, he has authored *Ossian Bingley Hart, Florida's Loyalist Reconstruction Governor* and *Florida's Black Public Officials, 1867-1924* and co-authored *Laborers in the Vineyard of the Lord: The Beginnings of the AME Church in Florida, 1865-1895*. He has received the Rembert Patrick Book Award of the Florida Historical Society, the Southern Jewish Historical Society's B.H. Levy Prize, and the Certificate of Commendation of the American Association for State and Local History. He is a native of Fort Meade, Polk County, Florida.